Awareness Adventures

Discovering Your True Nature

Brian Tom O'Connor

Back cover photo by Josh Yu

Front cover photo by Adele Payman on Unsplash

Published by Slippery Mind

ISBN-13: 978-0-578-89210-8

www.playawarenessgames.com

For Josh

The entire adventure of the separate self takes place in a little bubble of thought and feeling within Awareness, but Awareness itself never takes the adventure.

— *Rupert Spira*

The only journey is the one within.

— *Rainer Maria Rilke*

Table of Contents

SETTING OUT

What if you heard about something that eased your pain, that soothed your suffering, that brought you joy and love and peace; something that overflowed with good humor and good will, that infused your every experience with beauty and grace and laughter? What if you heard that this something cost nothing, came in an infinite supply, and could never ever fail you?

What if the tales you heard of this marvelous something were so convincing that no doubt of its reality lingered in your mind?

How far would you travel to find it? How persistently would you search for it? How much would you value it if you found it?

What an adventure that would be!

Your voyage of discovery begins here.

The Catch

But there's a catch. Actually, a couple of catches. For one, this something is not a thing. For another, you don't have to travel any distance away from yourself to find it.

The mind can't fully understand it and words can't fully describe it. But it can somehow be known, and felt, and sensed, like a perfume from an unseen source.

It is awareness itself. Everyday garden-variety awareness. Always available, just waiting to be noticed, hiding under the veils of thinking, fixing, regretting, worrying.

Closer to you than your own breath. Actually, you couldn't even say it's close to you; it's closer even than that. So close to you, in fact, that it *is* you. But not the you that you take yourself to be, that is, your body, mind, and personality. It's what's looking out through your eyes right now. It's what knows you have a body. It's what all experience appears to.

Even better, it's not just you—it's everybody. Everything. The infinite singular universe experiencing itself through you and through everyone simultaneously.

Everything appears in it and therefore it allows everything choicelessly. Which is why its nature is unconditional love. It is happiness itself. It is the real you, looking out through the mask of what you take yourself to be—your personality, your body, your mind. It's love itself. It's happiness itself. *You* are love. *You* are happiness.

And the other catch is that none of this is absolutely true. None of these words can adequately describe pure awareness because it's beyond words. Words—those handy little tools of limitation— make distinctions that appear in relative reality but don't exist in deep ultimate reality, which is one undivided energy temporarily appearing as separate beings and objects. Much like whirlpools are temporary forms that are not separate from the water in which they appear.

But the beauty part is that you don't have to believe any theory or dogma or concepts in order to connect with the universal sea of joy. All you have to do is play in it. You play with whatever ways work for you in turning your attention from the contents of awareness to pure awareness itself. This is where the goodies are, not in the ideas, concepts, philosophies, metaphysics, or even ideals of self-improvement.

Intellectual understanding can sometimes help with experiential understanding, but it's not sufficient, and it can sometimes draw us into a never-ending morass of conceptualization. Experiential understanding, however, *is* sufficient and can occur without intellectual understanding. You can bring it about through imagination, self-inquiry, or awareness games that you play with your mind.

A Note About Exploring for Yourself

In this book, stuff to read and think about is found in regular paragraphs. Stuff to try for yourself and play around with is found in bulleted paragraphs. When you come across bullet points, take that as an invitation to look within, try the steps, play around with them, and see for yourself what they are pointing to.

I usually refer to the shorter bulleted sections as *explorations,* and the longer ones as *meditations,* with a few of the most playful ones designated as *games.* The explorations and games are meant to be played at any time for as short or long a duration as you like. The meditations are meant as longer dives into awareness. You can approach the meditations in several ways: 1) Read the text and follow along in your imagination. 2) Have a friend read the steps aloud to you as you follow along with eyes closed (or open if you prefer). 3) Record the steps on your phone or other recording device and play them back as you follow along in your imagination.

A fourth possibility may or may not be ready as you read this: listen to the audiobook version of *Awareness Adventures* when it comes out.

In addition, many of the meditations are available on YouTube in the playlists, "Brian Tom O'Connor Meditations" and "Meditations from Awareness Explorers."

In any case, approach the explorations, the games, and the meditations with the same attitude of playfulness and exploration.

In Appendix B you'll find lists of all the methods broken down by type and length. (See page 154.)

A Little Bit of Background

As readers of my first book, *Awareness Games* know, "be the background" is one of my favorite phrases. Of course, I'm talking about the background to all experience—pure awareness, where love and joy live.

But here, I thought I'd talk a bit about background in another sense: how I came to discover that awareness is the secret of happiness, hiding in plain sight in the pure background of all experience. So here goes.

Back in the 90s, I was acting in a production of *The Cherry Orchard,* and after the show closed, I was hit by yet another round of agonizing depression. (Okay, it *was* Chekhov.) It was a really good production, but after it closed, this feeling of helplessness and hopelessness descended upon me. Had it furthered my career? Had it gotten me an agent or some good reviews I could use? Had it brought me artistic fulfilment?

Of course, it was not the first time depression hijacked my life, but I thought I was over it. Throughout my teens, 20s, and 30s I had suffered severe bouts. And it wasn't just depression. It was a dark angry mass of pain that kept me at times reclusive, hostile, withdrawn, and defensive. There were periods of light between the storms, and during those times I was able to have some semblance of a working life and often a creative, artistic one, but the tyrannical beast of depression would drag me down whenever I got too close to a genuine productive life.

Many years of therapy had helped take the edge off depression and keep suicide at bay, but they hadn't really gone all the way to eradicating it.

In my case, it seems to have been a combination of suppressed anger (a key ingredient of depression), and a feeling of paralysis when faced with the prospect of furthering my acting career in the face of a debilitating and irrational fear of agents, casting directors, and anyone behind a desk (going back to early traumatic experiences at school).

I thought to myself, "Oh no, not again! I never want to be depressed ever again. I need to be a different sort of person from the person I am. How can I change?"

So, during some down time at my day job (which I was somehow able to hold down for almost 20 years, but which held no passionate interest for me), I searched on the internet for this: "How do people change?"

This led me on a wild ride of intriguing possibilities to explore, mostly involving magical thinking of some sort. I looked into various alternative forms of psychotherapy, various new-age techniques, hypnosis, NLP, even ritual magic (I admit with some embarrassment). Then I read a book about codependence, which suggested that, in order to become psychologically healthy, a person really needs to engage in some sort of spiritual practice. That idea intrigued me, so back to the web I went, searching for spirituality and spiritual practice. This led to investigations into meditation, Buddhism, chanting, Kabballah, Sufism, brain-wave entrainment (yes, this was billed as a spiritual practice), Gnosticism, A Course in Miracles, and other mystical traditions.

Oddly enough, it was on the brain-wave entrainment site, which posted book reviews from time to time, that I first heard about the great mid-twentieth century sages, Nisargadatta Maharaj, author of *I Am That,* and Ramana Maharishi, who was famous for teaching self-inquiry, asking "Who am I?" Bingo. It was about inner identity, not about external events and personality. I was so taken with the ideas of these guys that I knew where my heart lay at last.

So I began to search for any contemporary teachers following this path, and discovered there were a whole host of teachers and writers who pointed to the source of happiness within—many of whom published books, and some of whom came to New York City regularly to give talks. The first talk I attended was given by Pamela Wilson, a luminous and lovely teacher, whose talk was greeted with so much friendly laughter, that afterwards she referred to it as "sit down comedy." Other folks came to New York over the years, including Catherine Ingram, Neelam, Wayne Liquorman, Gangaji, David Dasarath Davidson, Adyashanti, Stuart Schwartz, Loch Kelly, and Rupert Spira, and I was lucky to be able to hear them. (Loch Kelly lived and taught in New York, then moved to California for a while, and then moved back to New York. When he came back, he said of NYC—channeling Frank Sinatra—"If you can wake up there, you'll wake up anywhere.")

The irony was, none of these teachers taught the one thing that I started my search to discover: *how people change.* Acceptance and allowing was the focus of their teaching, not self-improvement, or success, or achievement. I came to understand that happiness did not lie in the perfection of the personality, but in something much larger than personality—the spacious awareness in which all experience appears.

⤚

It wasn't just an intellectual understanding of their concepts, however. When I actually started to look for myself into the nature of who's doing the looking, with each exploration, little by little, a sort of "happy for no reason" feeling would come over me. With practice I discovered I could tap into this uncaused joy at any time; it was always available. Unless of course, I was trying to make the feeling happen because I didn't want to be experiencing the current feeling.

In those cases, as soon as I realized I was trying to make something happen instead of allowing whatever was arising, I would relax, let go of trying to change my experience, and the joy would come flooding back. A paradox. Stop trying to change experience, and experience changes.

I also discovered that even in the darkest onslaught of turbulent emotions, I could also access the joy of awareness, but only if I relaxed enough to allow the emotions to flow freely. Physical relaxation was just as important as mental relaxation. Emotions get stuck in a seemingly permanent eddy of spinning suffering, but it's the clutching against them that causes the suffering, not the emotions themselves. It's the attempts to get rid of them or prevent them that keep them spinning inside you. They *want* to flow out if you'd only relax enough to let them.

These insights led to the discovery of the three key elements of awareness practice: 1) relaxation, 2) allowing experience to be just as it is, and 3) turning attention inward to awareness itself. Sometimes I call them collectively "RAA," for Relaxing, Allowing, and "Aware-ing." (See "The Staff of RAA" later in the book.)

One big thing I discovered though, was that I was not good at traditional meditation. I was simply not disciplined enough to sit in a specific practice such as breath counting, mantra repeating, or flame gazing for long periods of time and at specific times of day. It simply wasn't the nature of this personality.

At first, I was in despair over this. I wondered, "How could I ever become simply happy, much less enlightened, if I don't even have the type of personality to stick to a daily meditation practice?" Again, circling back to how can I change myself.

This despair could have continued to spiral into suicidal depression, but instead, coupled with a stubborn determination to find happiness, it led me to this insight: hoping to change myself, trying to improve myself, wishing I were a different sort of person *was* in fact the obstacle to happiness. I needed to come to this insight over and over again, but finally, it stuck, and it opened the door to the happiness that is already there, inherently present in my true nature, and, I believe, that of everyone else's. The happiness that lies in the background of all experience—awareness itself.

But how to access awareness repeatedly and consistently? I was determined that I could find happiness even with my lack of discipline. Along with the discovery that I didn't have to change or fix myself, also came the discovery that I didn't have to change the nature of how I respond to meditative techniques. (Don't get me wrong. I have nothing against meditation. I still meditate. I love to meditate. It's just that now I meditate *whenever* I want to meditate, because I *want* to meditate, and for however *long* I want to meditate.)

Ever since I was a little kid, I used to play with my mind. For example, I used to lie awake in bed thinking the thought "what if there was nothing?" I would repeat and repeat this thought until a spooky sensation would come over me. A sort of a half mental, half physical sensation arising from the impossibly paradoxical idea that if there was nothing, there would be no one to experience nothingness. It wasn't a scary-spooky kind of feeling, it was more like a cool-spooky kind of feeling, and I wanted more of it.

Another game I used to play with my mind is what I later called "The Pencil Game." In my mind's eye, I would imagine a pencil standing vertically on its point, and then try to imagine it not falling down. Then I would try to imagine it lying flat but staying down without popping back up by itself. I was amazed that try as I might, my mind had other ideas, and the mental pencil would either fall down when I tried to imagine it standing on end, or, when I tried to imagine it staying down, it would pop back up all by itself! This little childhood game was a major hint for a couple of later insights. First, perhaps the mind is not utterly under our control, and second, maybe there's a deeper me that is aware of the mind's activity.

As an adult searching for happiness, I came to realize that this inherent playfulness was just as good as traditional discipline for cracking the secret of joy within. For instance, I would play around with the thought, "what if I had no intention?" and repeat it inwardly until a sort of giddy laughter would erupt, arising out of two things: the paradox of intending not to have an intention, and the simple joy of relaxing the mind's ceaseless intention-filled effort.

My mom was an actress, and she also ran theater groups for kids in grade school and later for high school age kids. One of the mainstays of her teaching was a suite of "theater games" which were developed by Viola Spolin of the Second City theater troupe in Chicago. These theater games were ways of improvising around a specific task, with the aim of enriching and enlivening the interaction between characters before getting down to rehearsing the actual text of a play. Many years later, it struck me that I could wed the idea of theater games with my playful approach to meditation, and I came up with *Awareness Games,* which became the topic of my first book.

Over time, playing around in this way deepened my experience of "the one who is looking" and the joy of being awareness began to permeate my life, even during times when I was not actively experimenting or playing awareness games.

I went from being severely depressed, hostile, and reclusive to being happy, joyful, and open, simply through playing around with being the clear background awareness, and not trying to fix or improve myself in any way.

I still have occasional problems, bad habits, all sorts of emotions and fears, but I've come to know that these are clouds passing through the open sky, and the sky is always there. The sky is the natural state of happiness, and it's there *even when* emotions, fears, problems, bad habits, and even neuroses arise. All I have to do is notice the sky of pure awareness, and see *it* as my true self. It's such a weird paradox: happiness is here even when you're feeling unhappy.

After writing *Awareness Games* and teaching them for a few years, deeper insights and new games would pop into view, so I've gathered them here and offer them for your enjoyment, edification, and illumination.

Spiritual Advertising

There are many attainments that are written and talked about in spiritual circles which basically seem to have no chance of happening for me. (I'm not a Type A personality when it comes to self-improvement or spiritual attainment. If you are, feel free to skip this section.)

The mind stops all of a sudden? What's the chance of that happening?

Meditate two to four hours every day? What's the chance I'll be able to stick to that?

Clearing my chakras of karmic knots? What's the chance of that happening for me?

Merging with the Divine?

Manifesting all that I desire?

Attaining nirvana, moksha, enlightenment?

Not impossible, but also not likely. Yes, many people have reported these lovely accomplishments, but they are the elite, the few, the fortunate—not the ordinary guy or gal like me. And when we hear of these things and revel in them, and dream of them happening to us, we forget that we're talking about a very small sample. We're not hearing about all the folks who engaged in the same practices, but for whom these events and accomplishments didn't happen.

The fundamental technique of advertising is to make you feel that there is something that you lack, or something that you need, or something that you have to fix, or something that's wrong with you, your household, your family, or the world. And then to offer you the solution, which, of course, you'll have to pay for.

What if there is nothing that needs to be fixed, nothing that needs to change? What if everything you seek is already here, simply waiting for you to notice?

That's pure awareness. It's not something that will happen tomorrow. It's not something that will be achieved if you have enough discipline. It's not something that you will attain if only you work hard enough or are good enough.

In fact, I believe this is the biggest misunderstanding in all of meditation. The misunderstanding is that we are attempting to get good at something in order to create a state that we don't have. But it's not the attainment of the state, or the improvement of the concentration, or the refinement of the technique, that contains the benefit. It's simply that *the attempt alone refocuses the direction of your attention from without to within,* or from the foreground to the background, or from the content of awareness to pure awareness itself. If you can redirect the focus of your attention at any given moment, you don't need to achieve some state, or perfect some technique, or break some sort of endurance record. You simply look, notice what's already there, and rest as that.

So ignore the ads. Turn away from the shiny promises, turn around and look inside for what's looking, and then turn around again and look out from there, knowing that you *are* that pure, choiceless, timeless, allowing, loving, infinite, unchanging, awareness that's already here and has always been here.

You don't have to do a single blessed thing, except notice it.

THE SEARCH

"Happiness is the only thing we seek for its own sake."

~Rupert
Spira

Looking for Happiness Where it Is, Not Where it Isn't

Everyone on Earth is seeking happiness whether they know it or not. When people seek nice things to buy, they're looking for the happiness they think those things will give them. When people seek exciting experiences, they're seeking the happiness that comes from the fun of those experiences and the memories they leave. When people seek relationships with other people, they're looking for the happiness they think the other person should be able to make them feel.

But we're looking for happiness where it isn't, instead of where it is.

First, let's consider where it *isn't:*

Happiness isn't in outside circumstances, or in thoughts, or in things we can acquire, relationships we can enjoy, experiences we can savor, or success we can achieve. It's not anywhere outside of us, or in any object that we can think of. It's not in the past, nor is it in the future. It's not in anything we can conceive of, nor in anything we can give a name to. These are all objects, and they come, and they go, and they don't contain happiness, and have no power to convey happiness. Enjoyment, yes. True lasting happiness, no.

Now let's look at where it *is:*

It's in the clear open choiceless background of pure awareness. We can say that it's inside of us, but even that isn't quite right. Looking inside of us is certainly the right place to start, but we're not looking inside of us for a thing; we're looking inside of us for what's looking. In other words, what is it that's looking out of our eyes, that's knowing our thoughts, that's experiencing our feelings, that's seeing the world, that's the same as it has always been ever since we were a little kid? It's our very selves.

Why is happiness found in pure awareness? Because pure awareness is choiceless. In other words, it doesn't decide what will appear in it and what won't. It's like a clear mirror. A mirror doesn't say, "I think I'll reflect that hat, but I don't like the color of that tie. I don't think I'm going to reflect it today." Awareness is simply aware. Aware of everything that appears in it—all images, all sounds, all sights, all objects, all thoughts, all feelings, all bodily sensations, all other people, the world. Awareness holds all these without choice, without judgment, without a desire to change anything, and this is the essence of unconditional love.

So when we look inside of ourselves for pure awareness— simple, everyday, garden-variety awareness—the open field of being that we ourselves are, we connect with unconditional love. And that feeling, that aroma, that taste of unconditional love echoes back to us as pure happiness.

The reason we don't connect with the happiness and joy of pure awareness, is that it's veiled by our thoughts about the past and the future, and the things we need to fix, and the problems we need to solve, and the things that are wrong with ourselves and the world, and the feelings we wish we didn't have, and the painful memories we wish we could avoid.

In other words, the flow of thoughts and problem-solving is so strong that it creates a one-way current. The joy inherent in the pure background of choiceless awareness can't flow through to our conscious mind because it's fighting that strong one-way current of thinking thinking thinking, fixing fixing fixing.

But connecting to that pure background is a little bit tricky. We're so used to sending our attention to words or to objects, that we don't have the muscle memory to turn attention around to the background of our experience, and around again to look out from there. So we need to play around with it and try different things and see which works best for us. This makes us the experts of our own awakening.

To help us, we need some tricks to calm the one-way current, some games we can play with our minds, and some explorations to find and connect to the joy that's in the background, just waiting to flow forward into our experience.

Here are some basic tricks or games or explorations to try:

We need to walk ourselves back from the content of our awareness, back and back and back to the clear screen on which everything appears.

Here's a quick way
- Look inside.
- Go inside.
- Go as far back as you can.
- Turn around.
- Look out from there.
- Be what's looking out from there.
- Know that all experience appears in you—the one who is looking out from there.

An even quicker way
- Ask yourself, "Who or what is noticing my body?"
- Whoever it is, or whatever it is, it's not your body. It's you, yes, but it's not your body. So then, who or what are you?

Here's a more detailed way. We can use a series of questions to walk ourselves back:

Exploration: Three-Step Walk-Back
Walk yourself back to your true self

- First, start with the contents of awareness.
    - Without attempting to change anything that's arising, take an inventory of everything that appears right now in this moment.

- What sounds am I hearing? Maybe there's traffic outside or the sound of an air conditioner or heater, or birds, or wind, or rain.
- What sensations am I feeling in my body? Maybe the feeling of my feet on the floor, or the weight of my body against the chair, or a breeze on my skin, or a rumbling in my stomach, or an itch, or an ache.
- What images are appearing before my eyes? If my eyes are closed, what abstract shapes are dancing against a black field?
- What thoughts are flowing through my mind?
- What feelings or emotions are flowing through my body?

  o Remember, it's very important that while you're playing with this, to make absolutely no attempt to change anything in your experience whatsoever. including how you feel, what you're thinking, and what anyone else is doing at this moment. At least for the duration of this exploration. You can always return to controlling your experience and the world later, if you really want to.

- Second, ask yourself what are all these appearing in, or to?
  o What is the silence that sounds appear in?
  o What is the empty field that sensations appear in?
  o What is the blank page that thoughts are written on?
  o What is this awareness that everything appears in?
     - Does it have any qualities of its own?
     - Has it been there all my life?
     - Does it have any limits?
     - What is its nature?
- Third, ask yourself, "what is aware?"
  o If the answer you come up with is "I am. I'm experiencing all these things. All these experiences are appearing to me," ask yourself what is this me?

- o Is it my body? Well maybe, but I notice that I have a body. I can experience my body. Who experiences it?
- o Then ask yourself, "What is this 'me' that notices all my experience?" And notice that anything that you can think of is an object that can be experienced, so it can't be the experiencer, it can't be you.
- o Who are you? What is this "me"?

I hope you see how these sorts of explorations are ways of looking in the exact opposite direction from where we usually look for happiness. It's not where you think it is. It's not where you think at all. It's where you look from.

The Awareness Compass
Instead of North, South, East, West—In, Back, Down, Out

It's natural that when we think of exploring, we think of traveling great distances to far-off places, or at least of giving our attention to something outside of ourselves.

When we explore something—anything—from countries we've never visited to the inner workings of objects we'd like to understand better, we are, naturally, asking questions. What is the nature of this place, or thing, or phenomenon? What's it like? How does it work? What's it made of? We direct our attention outward from ourselves toward that place or thing or phenomenon.

But the purpose of asking the questions in this book is never to come up with an answer. The purpose is to point your attention in the right direction.

What is the right direction? Here are the four directions of the Awareness Compass. Any will do.

In: Turn your attention inward from the content of awareness to awareness itself.

Back: Sink into the background. Be the space in which your experience appears.

Down: drop below the neck, away from the thinking mind and into the direct experience of your body.

Out: Expand ever outward so that everything that you could possibly experience—including your body, mind, and personality—is simply something that's known by something bigger, more expansive, and all-inclusive. You are not *going* out; you're *growing* out—expanding out—and becoming vaster and vaster until you are literally everything.

It's important to distinguish this last direction from the usual sense of the word "out." It's not the typical search for happiness involving something to get from "out there." You're not looking for something outside of yourself; you're expanding yourself so that everything appears in you.

The Staff of RAA
Relaxing, Allowing, Aware-ing
(Or, Rest As Awareness)

Whenever you feel anxious or overwhelmed or anything you'd rather not be feeling, remember RAA:

Relaxing

Allowing

Aware-ing

Relaxing:
- Check your body to see if there is any clutching or holding or tension, and take a breath.

Allowing:
- Just for a moment, ask if you can allow the feeling to be here. Just acknowledge that it's present.

Aware-ing:
- Notice the clear empty field in which the feelings appear. And in which everything else appears. And which is already present and is already allowing, because that's its nature.
- Be that knowingly. Rest As Awareness.

If you try this often enough, pretty soon you'll be able to simply say "RAA" and all of that will happen together.

Note that the last part, aware-ing, has two steps: *noticing* awareness and *being* awareness. Or if you like, two turnarounds: First you turn around from outside to inside. That is, you turn your attention from the content of awareness to awareness itself—from what is noticed to what is noticing. Second, you turn around again, towards the outside world, and look from there *as* awareness. Being awareness. (I could have called it RAAB--for Relaxing, Allowing, Aware-ing, and Being Awareness—but with practice, these last two parts start to feel like one movement—Aware-ing.)

Try the next three practices to experience each RAA element more fully.

Game Break: Tension Detective

Here's an imagination game that can help you relax. Any method of relaxation that you like can work for you, including the "Clutch Gobbler" game in *Awareness Explorers,* so if you already have a favorite, use that. If not, here's one that I enjoy.

- Close your eyes, sit comfortably, and take a few slow, easy, deep breaths.
- Imagine an inner detective with a magnifying glass combing your body from head to toe, looking for tension.
- He's looking for tension in your body the same way Sherlock Holmes might scour a room for clues.
- Start with the inside of your head just behind your forehead, and imagine the Tension Detective looking for tension.
- Imagine that when he finds a bit of tension or clutching, he says "Aha!" Then he picks up the bit of tension, puts it in his pocket and lets out a sigh of relief, saying, "Ahhh."
- Move to behind your eyes, and continue to imagine the detective finding tension, saying "Aha!" putting it in his pocket, and saying "Ahh," with a sigh of relief.
- Continue down to your mouth and jaw area, imagining the same "Aha!—Ahhh." Scenario.
- And down to your neck and shoulders...
- Aha! ... Ahhh.
- Down each arm, into your hands and back up...
- Aha! ... Ahhh.
- Down through your chest area...
- Aha! ... Ahhh.
- Your upper back...
- Your lower back...
- Your belly...

- Your hips and groin...
- Down each leg through your thighs, knees and calves...
- Into each foot, searching the ankles, heels, soles, toes...
- And go over the whole body one more time in case any tension was missed.
- Aha! ... Ahhh.

The beauty part is, you don't have to do the relaxing. The Tension Detective is doing it all for you.

Exploration: Just for Now

Once you're physically relaxed, the next step in awareness exploration is to allow everything to be as it is, just for now.

What does it mean to allow everything to be as it is? Does it mean that I should never say anything when I see injustice? Does it mean I should never attempt to improve myself or the world? Does it mean resigning myself to fate? No. That's past and future stuff. I'm just talking about now—just while you're sitting here—just for the duration of your current meditation, game, exploration, or practice.

Ask yourself these questions:

- Just for now, can I allow whatever I'm feeling to be here without a strategy to change it?
- Just for now, can I allow my body to feel and be just the way it is without a strategy to alter it?
- Just for now, can I allow my personality to be just the way it is without a strategy to improve it?
- Just for now, can I allow my thoughts to be just the way they are without attempting to change or control them?
- Just for now, can I allow the world to be just the way it is without a strategy to fix it?

Just for now, don't worry about what you need to do in the next few hours, days, or weeks. You can always return to worrying, changing, fixing, controlling, and strategizing later. Or not.

Meditation: Triangulation
Sounds plus Sensations plus Thoughts

There is nothing that you can experience that's not *experienced* in awareness. You can take this a step further and say that there is nothing that you can experience that does not *take place* in awareness. Which means, of course, that nothing *exists* outside of awareness.

In the first sentence above, there still could be something outside of, and therefore separate from, awareness. Something that exists even when we aren't aware of it. To most of us, awareness is like a camera. If we take a picture of a tree, the actual tree exists apart from the image of the tree in the camera. But unlike a camera, awareness is present in everything we perceive. There is simply nothing that can be perceived, known, or felt that can be perceived, known, or felt *apart from* awareness.

Awareness is the one thing common to all phenomena. And all phenomena consist of awareness. And the awareness with which we know various phenomena, like sights, sounds, sensations, thoughts, feelings, and perceptions—is not a different awareness for each. There is only one awareness, and it includes everything that is known or could ever be known.

But even if you don't *believe* any of this intellectually, you can still get a feel for the all-inclusive nature of awareness, and this can lead you into realizing the all-inclusive nature of your true self.

One of the best ways to experience the all-inclusiveness of awareness is to notice that more than one mode of experience appears in the same field of awareness at the same time. Here's a meditation for this, in which you notice three different modes of experience simultaneously.

- Take an easy deep breath and notice if there is any tension, holding, or clutching in your body, and gently let them soften and relax.
- Starting with your eyes closed, listen to the sounds around you—the hum of an air conditioner or heater, or perhaps

the sounds of traffic or birds or wind outside, or the sound of my voice.

- o   As you notice the sounds that appear, ask yourself, "What is the silent field in which the sounds appear?"
- o   Notice each sound separately, and ask the question, "What is the silent field in which this sound appears?"
- o   Now see if you can notice all the sounds at the same time, and ask yourself, "Do all the sounds appear in the same silent field?"

• Then notice your bodily sensations—the feel of your body on the chair, or your feet on the floor. Perhaps a breeze on your skin, or the rise and fall of your belly as you breathe.
- o   As you notice the sensations that appear, ask yourself, "What is the empty spacious field in which sensations appear?"
- o   Notice each sensation separately, and ask the question, "What is the empty spacious field in which this sensation appears?"
- o   Now see if you can notice all the sensations at the same time, and ask yourself, "Do all these sensations appear in the same empty spacious field?"

• Now see if you can notice both sounds and body sensations at the same time.
- o   Ask yourself, "Is the field in which sounds appear, the same as the field in which sensations appear?" This is the clear field of awareness.

• Notice what thoughts are appearing now.
- o   Imagine the thoughts are coming from somewhere outside of you and are projected on a blank screen inside you.
- o   Imagine that the screen has both sound and subtitles, so you can either hear or read each thought that appears.
- o   Imagine this screen is like a clear empty field in which thoughts appear.

- o As you notice the thoughts that appear, ask yourself, "what is the blank empty field in which these thoughts appear?"
- o Notice a few thoughts separately, as they appear in a sequence of thoughts, and for each one, ask yourself, "Do all these thoughts appear in the same empty field?"

- Now see if you can notice both the thoughts and the body sensation at the same time, and ask yourself, "Is the field in which thoughts appear, the same as the field in which sensations appear?"

- Then see if you can notice both the thoughts and the sounds at the same time, and ask yourself, "Is the field in which thoughts appear, the same as the field in which sounds appear?"

- Now see if you can notice all three—the sounds, the sensations, and the thoughts—appearing at the same time, and ask yourself, "Are these all appearing in the same clear empty field of awareness?"

- That field is your true nature. Clear, spacious, silent, allowing,

- Now, if your eyes are closed, gently open them again and take another easy breath.

NOTE: Since this is a long guided meditation, it might be useful to have someone read this slowly to you out loud. Or you could record it into your phone in your own voice and play it back. Or you can listen to the audio version of this book when it comes out. Or you can listen to "The 'I' of My' Meditation" in the YouTube playlists, "Meditations from Awareness Explorers" or "Brian Tom O'Connor Meditations."

⚘

This meditation has been key for me in separating out awareness from its content. When I would try meditating on a sound or a mantra, or gazing at a stone, or watching my breath or my thoughts, the object of the meditation would always upstage awareness itself. But, when I compare different senses (and Buddhists consider thinking to be the sixth sense), and look for the common element among them, it's much easier for me to see that awareness is the same in every case.

After you have mastered this one, please try "Quadrangulation," which adds the sense of self to the one field of awareness.

Thought Experiments: Five (not so) Easy Pieces

Here are some ideas that will help anchor you during the flights into the clear sky of awareness that follow. If you find while reading them that there's smoke coming out of your brain, you can always jump to the next section, "A Quiet Adventure."

1. Consciousness is not Local

A lot of philosophers and scientists are attempting to understand consciousness right now. Most start with the assumption that each of us has our own individual consciousness that somehow exists in our individual brains. Some have asked this question, "how does the brain create consciousness?"

How do we know the brain *does* create consciousness? It's hard to imagine that this unexamined assumption can be the basis of a philosophy of consciousness.

What if consciousness is not local?

What if it's not *my* consciousness or *your* consciousness, but *the universe's* consciousness looking at itself through billions of pairs of eyes?

What if my body, my mind, your body, your mind, and the entire world are all appearing in one consciousness?

You don't have to believe it... just play with it and see if it shifts your sense of who you really are.

2. Adventures in Radical Nonduality

Nonduality is the philosophical and spiritual understanding of the oneness of all things. In other words, there is only one thing going on in the universe; only one fundamental reality out of which all appearances arise.

But this is a tricky idea and filled with paradox. To some, this means there is no such thing as duality. Which makes sense, since that's literally what the word *nonduality* means. Its Sanskrit forerunner, *advaita,* means "not two."

However, to deny duality is to misunderstand nonduality.

To deny duality is to ignore the paradox at the center of the mystery of nonduality: we are one energy, and we are separate forms of that energy. Both/And.

It's like a bow and arrow. The string must first be separated from the bow, in order for them to come together and send the arrow to its target.

We have to turn our attention from the content of awareness to the pure background awareness before we can then turn around again and look out at the world from there. That's when we can begin to see that not only are we and the world in awareness, but that we and the world are made of awareness.

That's why the idea that there is nothing to do is only one half of the paradox of truth. The other half of the paradox is that doing nothing takes practice. We don't come to it by the thought "there's nothing to do." Doing nothing ain't easy.

And yet it is easy. That's part of the paradox. It's not easy for your individual mind, but it's easy for awareness. In fact, it's beyond easy—it's the nature of awareness to do nothing. To be nothing. It's nothing because it has no qualities. Anything with qualities can be known by awareness, and therefore can't be awareness. On the other hand, because nothing exists outside of awareness (have you ever known anything outside of awareness?), awareness is everything. As Wayne Liquorman says, "Consciousness is all there is."

You can't ignore the paradox that there's nothing you can do and that you must turn your attention from the content to the background, and then be the background knowingly. You can't ignore the paradox that all is one and that we each are gloriously individual creations. In fact, recognizing your true nature as universal awareness mysteriously allows the individual personality to flourish and share its unique gifts.

To deny paradox is to miss the central insight of nondual awareness.

Nothing. Everything. Oneness. Multiplicity. Duality. Nonduality. Embrace the paradox.

3. Enlightenment vs. Happiness

In some ways, it's agonizing to search for enlightenment. It seems forever to remain in the future—something desired but ungraspable; always something we hope will happen to us in a tomorrow that never arrives.

But the main reason we started looking for enlightenment was because we wanted to be happy! And now we make ourselves unhappy because some future event called "enlightenment" or "awakening" hasn't yet occurred. This is so unnecessary! Especially when happiness is available right now, right here, and is always available twenty-four-seven, no matter what.

Happiness is available right now in the mirror-like spaciousness of pure awareness, which is what everything that's appearing is appearing in. Like a mirror, it's choiceless; it doesn't decide to include the table and not the chair. It's unconditional love. It's the empty background of all appearance. It's joy and acceptance and happiness itself. Pure awareness is your true self, and it never lets you down. It's open to all experience, good and bad, painful and pleasurable, turbulent and peaceful, anxious and calm, objectionable and praiseworthy—in fact, even happy or sad. Awareness is happy even when you're sad. How's that for a paradox?

So there doesn't have to be an event in the future, a crash of cymbals and rattle of drums, for us to discover joy and peace and love and happiness. It's here now. Now. Here. This.

"But," you may protest, "I don't want what's here now to be the way it is! I don't want this to be happening! I don't want to be the way I am. I don't want other people to act the way they do!" Even those feelings are appearing in pure awareness completely without resistance. In awareness, resistance is not resisted. The screen is not affected by the movie playing on it.

So don't wait for enlightenment. Be the screen, be the background, ease out the clutching against the way things are, go on an adventure, look for yourself, and uncover the infinite well of joy behind all experience, good, bad, or ugly.

4. Consciousness vs. Awareness
Adventures in semantics

Some teachers equate consciousness and awareness and treat them synonymously. This works fine most of the time, but sometimes can lead to confusion.

Some say consciousness is what awareness appears in. To me, this also leads to unnecessary confusion.

The confusion stems from the different usages of the term consciousness. Spiritual seekers and teachers define it as the infinite mysterious force pervading everyone and everything. Philosophers of mind may define it as the ability to experience—or what "it is like" to be a particular conscious organism. In addition, the common usage refers to consciousness as that which disappears when we are under anesthesia or in deep sleep. The terms "knocked unconscious" or "regain consciousness" illustrate this usage.

So I propose an alternative way of thinking, which is neither to think of them synonymously, nor to think of awareness as somehow a subset of consciousness, but instead, accept the common—and even medical—usage of the word consciousness, and make a different distinction between the two terms—one that is actually the opposite of the "awareness as a subset of consciousness" model.

Let's say we define consciousness as that which disappears when we are under anesthesia or in deep sleep. If so, we can define awareness as that from which consciousness disappears.

It may be helpful to substitute the term, "sensory input" for "consciousness" when used in this sense. In other words, when we are in deep sleep or under anesthesia, what disappears is sensory input, not awareness.

This way, we can understand awareness as something that never disappears even when consciousness, now understood as a local phenomenon, disappears. Similar to a screen that doesn't disappear when no movie is projected on it, or a TV set that doesn't disappear when the power is turned off. Awareness is still there, but the light of local consciousness, that is, sensory input, has been temporarily turned off, or at least reduced to a minimum. In other words, consciousness appears in awareness and consciousness is simply the input into awareness which can be turned on or off.

On the other hand, perhaps sensory input does not completely disappear during deep sleep, but is only drastically reduced. Have you ever been awakened by an alarm clock or by someone shaking you awake during a deep sleep cycle? This would not be possible if awareness was absent during deep sleep.

As Rupert Spira says, "Deep sleep is not the absence of awareness, but the awareness of absence."

This understanding can help us to realize that awareness is a non-local phenomenon.

I believe that in philosophical and neuroscientific studies of consciousness, the misunderstanding of the distinction between two definitions of consciousness—that is, that in which our experience occurs, on the one hand, and that which disappears during deep sleep or under anesthesia, on the other hand—is an obstacle to understanding consciousness as non-local, infinite, and universal, as opposed to a phenomenon occurring in, and generated by the mind or the brain.

This obstacle is at the core of the so-called "hard problem of consciousness," and the argument over the assumption that the brain creates consciousness. Yes, the brain does seem to create consciousness if we accept the common usage definition of consciousness as that which disappears under anesthesia. No, the brain does not create consciousness if we accept the definition of consciousness as that which knows our experience. That which knows our experience is non-local, universal, infinite, ever-present.

I call it awareness. You can call it consciousness, or knowingness, or the witness, or whatever you like, as long as you understand that it is greater than—but includes—everything that you take yourself to be, including your body, your brain, your mind, your ego, or your personality.

5. Seeking a Purpose

If you're talking about the ultimate purpose, then we can't know what it is. On the other hand, the question alone implies that there is some entity apart from ourselves that has a purpose for us. Which is not possible, since there is nothing separate from us... us meaning infinite consciousness—that which is looking out of all of our eyes.

However, there appears to be something very much like a purpose for each individual. We see this in the flourishing of our individual personalities. Each of us has a set of talents and natural proclivities, which, when they are nurtured and developed can lead to a sense of well-being—a feeling that "I'm doing what I'm meant to be doing." And when they are stifled or suppressed, we feel stuck and isolated from the natural flow of things.

We also see this in our desires. Because when we have emotions and desires, there is indeed a purpose behind them. And that purpose is to feel better, to seek happiness. But if we look behind its disguise, that desire for happiness is the desire to know ourselves as infinite awareness and remove the sense of separation. Contrary to our knee-jerk instinct that creating boundaries makes us safer, it's the sense of separation that causes us to feel unsafe, unprotected, far from home, and conversely, it's the knowing of our true nature as the one universal energy looking out at itself through our eyes that causes us to feel love, to feel safe, to feel at peace and at home.

The problem is that we don't see through our immediate desires and discover that ultimate desire. Instead, we're distracted by the idea that we need to change something, that our desires mean something is wrong, something needs to be fixed. We're distracted from the universal desire—the unveiling of the Infinite Oneness.

So when you find yourself wondering what your purpose is, start with the questions, "Am I happy? Am I at peace?" Because only inner peace can bring about outer peace, which the world so sorely needs. Isn't this purpose enough?

OK, that last section was a bit heady. Take a moment to catch your breath, and try the next exploration...

Exploration: Down the Rabbit Hole of Breath
Follow the breath inside

Here's a game you can play with your breath and travel within to find that secret Wonderland of awareness.

- Get comfy.
- Take some slow deep breaths.
- Follow each breath Inside yourself as you inhale, like Alice following the White Rabbit down the rabbit hole.
- Each breath takes you further down the rabbit hole into your deepest inner self.
- When you feel yourself relaxing more and more deeply into the rabbit hole, look around on the table and find the bottle labeled "Drink me."
- Take a breath, drink from the bottle, and feel yourself getting smaller and smaller.
- When you're satisfied that you're small enough, look around for a tea cake marked "Eat me."
- Take a breath, eat the cake, and find yourself growing larger.
- Imagine yourself growing larger until you fill the body you entered when you went down the rabbit hole.
- Imagine yourself getting larger than your original body, until you can look down and see your original body.
- Imagine yourself getting larger and larger and expanding and expanding until you fill the entire universe.

Game Break: See How Long You Can...
The basic prototype game

Often, we play games with ourselves like, "see how long I can hold my breath," Or "see how long I can stare without blinking." Some people play even more esoteric games like, "see how long I can *not* think of a pink elephant," or "see how long I can talk without using any form of the verb *to be.*"

Here are similar games you can play with awareness:

- How long can I...
    - ...go without thinking about the past?
    - ...go without thinking about the future?
    - ...go without judging or criticizing myself or anyone else?
    - ...go without any verbal thought?
    - ...keep my attention on awareness itself, instead of what I'm aware *of?*
    - ...go without labeling anything?
    - ...only think thoughts that are fun and feel good?

These are really the prototypes of Awareness Games, and really, meditation is simply a "how long can I" game.

For the one about going without verbal thought (meaning words in your head), instead of avoiding verbal thought, focus on what else is present in your awareness *other than* verbal thought. In other words, what can be experienced non-verbally? For example, the sounds in the room or outside, sensations—like a breeze or the weight of your body in a chair or a tingling in your hands or feet.

An important note about this game—and indeed, all the games, explorations, and meditations—is that you will lose most of the time. For instance, when you play with how long you can go without verbal thought, within seconds, verbal thoughts come in. The trick here is this: Don't put yourself down when this happens, congratulate yourself for catching it! Then simply let it go and return to noticing what's here without words or labels.

This is key: It's not the achievement of these goals that does the trick, it's simply the *attempt,* which redirects your attention from the unhappiness in the foreground of thought to the happiness in the background of awareness.

✍

I hope that using "how long can I" as a prototype will give you the same freedom I felt when I finally realized that I had to be my own experimenter. When I started to think of myself as the scientist who experiments on himself, instead of the student who must obey the rules of the teacher, I was able to jump-start my own practice. Who better but you to see inside yourself and determine what works for you?

Nothing Needs to Change

As I mentioned earlier, there is an idea in nondual circles that there is nothing to do in order to become enlightened or wake up to the truth. This leaves many people with the feeling of being painted into a conceptual corner.

If you are having difficulty with this, maybe instead of "there is nothing to do," the phrase, "Nothing needs to change" might be helpful.

The realization that nothing needs to change is a doing of a sort. It's noticing what's here now. And noticing that awareness is already here. It's already allowing. It's already all-inclusive. Nothing about you—about your personality, about your ego, about your body, about your relationships, about your activities, about your interactions with the world, about your thoughts—can change this simple fact. Awareness is already present, and it is already *you* in the deepest sense.

So the doing is the noticing of awareness itself. The doing is imagining, "what if there was nothing that needs to change in order for me to be pure awareness?"

A QUIET ADVENTURE

Ramana Maharshi, the great Indian sage of the twentieth century, asked us to find out where thoughts come from.

Most of us feel that we create our thoughts, but if that were true, wouldn't we be able to decide to think only the thoughts we'd like to think? Wouldn't we think only pleasant or happy or satisfying thoughts, and never choose to think a painful or stressful or upsetting thought?

Let's imagine, just for now, that we don't purposely generate thoughts, but that instead, they enter our minds from who knows where. Where is that where? Where do thoughts come from?

Thinking doesn't actually represent reality. At best it's a filtered version of reality, but most of the time it's like virtual reality. It's not what's happening here and now, it's an entirely imagined scenario made up of scenes from the past and the future, neither of which are real.

And yet, thinking might not be in your power to control. Thoughts come and go, unbidden. The key is to investigate to whom or to what the thoughts are appearing.

Quieting Your Mind

Thinking is a big issue that's talked about a lot in spiritual or meditation circles, and especially in regard to stopping your thinking or quieting your mind. But this is really difficult for most people to do, maybe even impossible. Perhaps there are wonderful adepts and yogis who can do that. And yet it's true that thinking can cause emotions that we may not want, and thinking and emotions can obscure the background of pure awareness in which they appear.

The tricky part, though, is that when you're trying to quiet the mind or to stop thinking, you're in a battle with the mind—you're trying to control it. And that battle, that conflict, is obscuring the background of pure awareness.

So I've found that no matter what I'm thinking, I just let myself think it, and notice the spaciousness, the space of pure awareness that the thinking is happening in.

This is where happiness lives.

So here are a bunch of explorations that help put thinking in perspective.

A Couple of Quick Thought Explorations

Try this:

- For a few minutes, don't attempt to control your thoughts; just let 'em come.
- Try to trace each thought from its appearance back to the place from which it arose.
- If it seems to you that thoughts enter your mind from someplace outside of you, then see if you can trace each thought back out to wherever it came from.
- If it seems to you that thoughts arise from some internal place into your mind, then see if you can trace each thought back into that internal place from which thoughts arise.
- See if you can feel into this place without actually thinking about it in words.
- Repeat as often as necessary until the thoughts start to get quieter or come less often with more space in between.

And speaking of the space in between thoughts, here's a time-honored technique to get a sense of the negative space of awareness that surrounds the foreground of thought:

- For a few minutes, don't attempt to control your thoughts; just let 'em come, and let 'em go.
- Notice that the thoughts come one after another, and there are spaces in between them during which no thought is appearing.
- As each thought comes and goes, see if you can notice the space in between each thought.
- Be that space in between thoughts.

What Is Thought?

What actually is thought anyway? Asking yourself this question takes the focus off the content of thought. The content of thought will never make you happy. It's simply not in its nature. It's nature is to lead you in the opposite direction, because it has one goal: to figure out what needs to change and how to change it.

But asking what thought *is* puts you outside of thought. That's where the real goodies are.

- What is thought?
- Where does it come from?
- What does it appear to?
- What's it made of?
- Does it happen by itself?

Remember, don't try to answer these questions with facts. That's for the neuroscientists. Don't try to answer these questions with logic. That's for philosophers. Don't even try to answer them with words. What we're about here is experimenting on yourself and inquiring into your direct experience. The questions above are designed to turn the focus of your mind around—from concepts to the space in which concepts appear.

And remember, the purpose of asking the questions in all of these games, explorations, and meditations is never to come up with an answer. The purpose is to point your attention in the right direction. And the right direction is back inside to what's noticing your experience.

To be outside of thought, you can't just create thought about thought—that's just more thought. Instead, you have to feel your way outside of thought, and be the thing that thought appears in. (Actually, the nothing that thought appears in.)

Exploration: Lace of Thought
Thinking of thoughts as like lace

- Visualize your thoughts as lace.
- Imagine that there are spaces through which the background can be seen.
- Even if you move the lace around, thereby calling attention to it, notice that the background can still be seen through the holes in the lace.

> The same with thought. Its constant movement draws attention, and it seems as if we can only see the interwoven thoughts in the foreground. But actually, the background is always visible.

- Notice the background through the holes in thought.
- Imagine moving the lacework of thought aside a little to see more of the background of awareness. Then move the lacework back and see if you can still notice the background even more clearly.

You don't have to get rid of the lace to know that the background is there. You don't have to get rid of thought to see that the background of awareness is always there.

Although the background is easier to see when the lace is still, with a little practice you can always see the background no matter what's happening with the lace of thought. Start by imagining moving the lace of thought aside, as in the last step above, then play with seeing through the lace without changing anything about the lacework of your mind.

Extra credit:
- If you can see the background through the lace, move to the other side of the lace, become the background, and look out through the lace at the world.
- Then remove the lace of thought and see the world as it truly is.

Game Break: Depth Charge
Exploding your thoughts

Notice you're thinking. Notice that thoughts come. Notice that sometimes the thoughts stick around as we spin them into bigger and more complex thoughts. In other words, we think about our thoughts, and they get bigger and bigger until they take over.

Here's a game you can play with your thoughts instead of spinning them.

- For each thought that comes into your head, imagine it's a depth charge (an explosive that's dropped into water, allowed to sink, and then explodes at a specific depth).
- Drop the depth charge from your head down through your neck into your heart.
- Imagine it exploding there. Imagine that the explosion dissolves it into smithereens.
- For each thought that comes, imagine it sinking down from your head into your heart and exploding.

If this seems too, well, explosive, simply imagine there is a deep pool of water in your heart, and each thought is a stone that drops and plunges into the pool, creating rings of silent ripples.

- For each thought that comes into your head, imagine it's a stone that's dropped into water and allowed to sink.
- Imagine the stone dropping from your head down through your neck into your heart.
- Imagine it sending ripples in every direction in the deep pool of your heart.
- Continue with each thought that comes, imagine it sinking down from your head into the deep pool of your heart and sending silent ripples in all directions throughout the universe.

HEART OF LIGHTNESS

As we learn to know ourselves as awareness itself, the next adventure is to awaken the spiritual heart, which is bigger than, and contains the physical and emotional heart. This is what helps us experience the intimate unity of all things, including ourselves, and opens us up to the unconditional love that is its very nature. Love increases as the sense of intimacy between us and "not us" increases, and the separation between subject and object dissolves. This is felt directly in the heart.

The Heart Meditation
Traveling from the mind to the heart and out to the world

This is a meditation of imagination. You don't have to believe anything; you just have to imagine it only for the duration of the meditation.

Part 1
- Start by looking around and noticing that your eyes are a sense organ.
  - In other words, light and images are coming into your eyes, and through them into awareness.
  - Just notice that what you see is appearing in awareness.
- Now close your eyes and notice your hearing.
  - Notice that your ears are a sense organ.
  - In other words, sounds are coming into your ears and through them into awareness.
  - Just notice that what you hear is appearing in awareness.
- Notice the thoughts that are coming into your mind.
  - Think of your mind as a sense organ.

- o In other words, thoughts come into your mind, and through it into awareness.
- o Just notice that your thoughts appear in awareness.
- Ask yourself. "Where is this awareness in which sights, sounds, and thoughts appear?"
  - o Since the eyes are in the head, and the ears are in the head, and thoughts seem to be in the brain, if you're like most people you will answer "in my head."
  - o If so, just notice or imagine awareness inside your head.
- Now, in your imagination, drop down from the head to below the neck.
- Notice the sensations on your skin.
  - o Perhaps there's a breeze. Or you can feel your shoes or the floor. Or with your hands you can feel the chair or the table.
  - o Notice your skin as a sense organ.
  - o In other words, sensations come through your skin and appear in awareness.
- Notice any other bodily sensations that are appearing right now, and notice the awareness in which they appear.
- Then ask, what if the heart was a sensory organ? What is appearing in it?
- What if everything that is appearing in all the other sensory organs is appearing in the heart?
- What if the heart was totally okay with everything that it experiences? With everything that appears in it? With everything that could ever appear in it?
- Imagine that your heart reflects everything that appears without choice, without exclusion.
  - o Imagine that it allows everything to be just as it is. Just for now. You can go back to excluding or not allowing later. If you want to.

- So just for now, imagine that your heart allows everything to be just as it is.
- Imagine that this allowing is the definition of love itself.
- Imagine your heart is love itself.
- Imagine your heart is you. You are love.

Part 2
What if the entire body appeared inside the heart?

- Imagine your heart expanding with love and allowing.
- Imagine your heart expanding to fill your entire chest.
- Imagine your heart expanding to fill your entire torso.
- Imagine your heart expanding outside of the boundaries of your chest and torso.
- Imagine your heart expanding so that it includes your entire body.
- Imagine that your heart loves your body and allows it to be exactly as it is.
- Imagine your heart expanding to fill the entire room.
- Imagine your heart expanding to include everyone you know and love.
- Imagine your heart expanding to include everybody you don't know or don't love.
- Just for now, imagine that everything in the world is so close to you, so intimate with you, that the boundary between you and everything in the world starts to dissolve.
- Imagine you are your heart, you are pure awareness, you are love, you are everything.

NOTE: Since this is a long guided meditation, it might be useful to have someone read this slowly to you out loud. Or you could record it into your phone in your own voice and play it back. Or you can listen to the audio version of this book when it comes out. Or you can listen to "Heart Meditation" in the YouTube playlists,

"Meditations from Awareness Explorers" or "Brian Tom O'Connor Meditations."

Game Break: Seeing from the Heart
Inner eyes

After you've experienced the Heart Meditation above, you can play this quick game as often as you think of it.

- With your eyes open, notice the sense of what's looking that seems to be in your head, behind your eyes.
- Close your eyes.
- Allow your attention to drop from the head to the heart area.
- Pour your attention into the heart.
- Open your eyes
- Look out at your immediate surroundings from the heart
- Imagine that it is your heart that is seeing the world.

The Joy of Being Awareness

Sat Chit Ananda is a term that has made its way into western popular culture from the Upanishads of Hinduism. I am no scholar of Hinduism, but the term is so often used in modern spiritual-type talk that it's become almost as common as *chakra, nirvana, dharma, karma, mantra,* or *yin and yang.*

Sat Chit Ananda is most often translated as "being, consciousness, bliss," and some translate it as "existence, understanding, happiness." *Sat* is often described as absolute truth or absolute being—that which never changes. Pure existence. *Chit* is often described as pure consciousness—"the ear of the ear, the mind of the mind, the eye of the eye." *Ananda* has been described as causeless joy, happiness for no reason.

Here's my experience: When I turn my attention around from the *content* of my experience to whatever is *aware* of experience, and then turn around once more and look out *at* experience *from* awareness itself, I'm flooded with joy. It's a joy unrelated to whatever is actually happening in my experience. It's a joy that seems as if it has always been there, and always will be there, waiting for me, steadfast and unchanging. It's a joy that's unaffected by the external experience. The act of looking out from awareness is the act of identifying *as* awareness, *being* awareness. I, Awareness.

So that's why, when I think of *Sat Chit Ananda,* I think of it as *the joy of being awareness.* I don't believe it's the lofty goal that the ancients have reserved for a select few. I don't believe it's a state that requires many years, or many lifetimes of meditation and purification to experience. I believe it's available right here, right now, to anyone. It's here when your mind is quiet and it's here when your mind is active. It's here when calmness prevails and it's here when all hell breaks loose, but we often don't notice it because noisy minds and frenzied activity grab all the attention.

But you can simply turn your attention away from thinking and struggle, and towards the calm, spacious, all-inclusive awareness that's already here, lovingly, patiently waiting for you.

I highly recommend it.
Meditation: Window to Eternity
Another Imagination Meditation

- Imagine that you are looking through a small hole, like a peephole in a wall, or a very small window looking into a construction site from the sidewalk.

- You are on one side of the hole and everything that you are seeing is on the other side of the hole.

- Now imagine that this very small peephole starts to expand and gets a little bit larger. At first you notice that as the hole gets larger, more and more of what can be seen comes into view.

- The hole is expanding and now it's the size of your head, and you can see more of what's on the other side of the hole.

- And now the hole is expanding more, and it's the size of your whole upper body. You can see huge vistas beyond the hole in all directions.

- And now the hole expands to the length and width of your entire body. You can see very far in almost every direction through the hole.

- Now imagine that as the hole continues to expand even more, the hole moves toward you so that it now surrounds your body on all sides, not just in front of your body.

- And now the hole expands and moves closer so that your entire body is part of the view that can be seen through this hole.

- As the hole continues to expand, it becomes a three-dimensional ring, or circle, or globe that includes everything that can be seen in any direction forward, backward, up, or down, and includes your body.

- So you are the view. You are the hole itself. You can see your body and everything that surrounds it within the view of this ever-expanding sphere-like hole.

- And now imagine that the hole expands even more and more and begins to include the landscape very far in every direction, as far as the eye can see, and all the while still includes your body in the view.

- And now imagine that as the hole gets even bigger and bigger—becoming the spherical space that sees everything, including yourself—it now encompasses and surrounds the entire world, including yourself, in the view.

- Now imagine that as it expands and expands, it includes the entire solar system, the entire galaxy, the entire universe.

- Become the entire universe seeing everything in its view, including you.

JOURNEY TO THE CENTER OF THE SELF

"Flow down and down
in always widening rings of being."
         ~ Rumi, from "A Community of the Spirit"

"Who Am I?" is the question Ramana Maharshi instructed his followers to ask, and this question is central to knowing yourself as awareness.

So who are you? What are you? Who or what is noticing your experience?

Is there anything you can think of that's not noticed by this mysterious something that notices all of your experience?

Anything you can think of or name, including your body, your mind, and your personality is noticed by something, so it cannot be that something. Or that nothing, if you prefer, since it has no qualities of its own. Anything with qualities can be noticed. What's noticing? I am. Who or what am I? Who notices that?

It's an infinite regression.

The mind can't really get it—that's not its job. But you can feel into it, play with it, and open to the indescribable source of it all—your own infinite self.

Because this whole thing about shifting identity and recognizing your true nature is such a key ingredient to natural happiness, I've included a whole slew of approaches to try. Here's an exploration, three longer meditations, and a couple of games, for you to play with.

Exploration: Nothing You Can Think of is You
Not this, not that

- Think of everything about yourself. And after each item ask yourself, "What's noticing this? Or, if you prefer, "What is this appearing in?" Or, if you prefer, "Who is aware of this?"
- Think of everything about yourself. For example...
  - My name. What's noticing my name?
  - My body. What's noticing my body?
  - My thoughts. What's noticing my thoughts?
  - My personality. What's noticing my personality?
  - My face. What's noticing my face?
  - My emotions. What's noticing my emotions?
  - My job or profession. What's noticing my job or my profession?
  - My mind. What's noticing mind?
  - My brain. What's noticing my brain?
  - My field of vision. What's noticing my field of vision?
  - My body sensations. What's noticing my body sensations
  - My age. What's noticing my age?
  - My gender. What's noticing my gender?
  - My talents. What's noticing my talents?
  - My abilities. What's noticing my abilities?
  - My faults. What's noticing my faults?
  - My flaws. What's noticing my flaws?
  - My expertise. What's noticing my expertise?
  - My knowledge. What's noticing my knowledge?
  - My spouse or partner or lack of one. What's noticing my relationship status?
  - My family. What's noticing my family?
  - My home. What's noticing my home?
  - My hair. What's noticing my hair?
  - Me. What's noticing me?

- After each one, ask, "Is this me? Or is there something larger that is aware of this? Is *that* me?"

Simply know that anything you can name in the above list, or *anything* about yourself that you can conceive of or name, is not you. Why? Because there is something else larger or more spacious that is aware of that item, and *that* larger spacious clear infinite something (which is actually nothing) is your real self, and indeed everyone's real self. The Universal Self that is aware of everything through every sensate being.

For a more detailed guided meditation version of this, see "The 'I' of 'My'," below.

Inquiry Meditation: The "I" of "My"
Who is this Me?

When we talk about parts of our bodies, we say things like, "my arm hurts," "my fingers are cold," "my foot is asleep," "my head aches." We even talk about "my body."

We know what we're referring to when we say, "arm," "fingers," "foot," "head," and even "body," but what does "my" refer to? Who is the "me" or "I" behind the "my"?

If we answer, "my body," who is this "me" who has a body?

If we answer, "my mind," who is this "me" who has a mind?

If we answer, "a thought," who has the thought? To whom does it appear?

Try this with various parts of your body, then try it with anything you could possibly conceive of as "I" or "me."

For example...

- Think, "my hand." Then ask yourself, "Who has a hand? Who is this 'me' who has a hand? What is the 'I' that 'my' refers to?"

- Think, "my face." Then ask yourself, "Who has a face? Who is this 'me' who has a face? What is the 'I' that 'my' refers to?"

- Then try it with...
  My head
  "Who has a head? Who is this 'me' who has a head? What is the 'I' that 'my' refers to?"

- My heart
  "Who has a heart? Who is this 'me' who has a heart? Who is the 'I' of 'my heart'?"

- My eyes
  "Who has eyes? Who is this 'me' who has eyes? Who is the 'I' of 'my eyes'?"

- My thoughts
  "Who has a thought? Who is this 'me' who has thoughts?"
- My name
  "Who has a name? Who is this 'me' who has a name?"
- My emotions
  "Who has emotions? Who is this 'me' who has an emotion?"
- My personality
  "Who has a personality? Who is this 'me' who has a personality?"
- My body
  "Who has a body? Who is this 'me' who has a body? Who is the 'I' of 'my body'?"
- My mind
  "Who has a mind? Who is this 'me' who has a mind? Who or what is the 'I' of 'my mind'?"
- My ego
  "Who has an ego? Who is this 'me' who has an ego? Who or what is the 'I' of 'my ego'?"
- Most people's strongest felt sense of who they ultimately are is one of these: my body, my mind, my thoughts, my ego, my name, or my personality. Pick the one that you most strongly feel is you, then repeat the questions above, focusing on that one, repeating it several times. Repeat it for as long as you like, or until you feel a shift in the felt sense of "I."

When you ask the questions, you're not looking for a logical or factual answer. You're not looking for an object or a thing. Rather, you're trying to feel into the sense of the ultimate "I" to which all objects, all things, and all experiences appear.

NOTE: Since this is a long guided meditation, it might be useful to have someone read this slowly to you out loud. Or you could record it into your phone in your own voice and play it back. Or you can listen to the audio version of this book when it comes out. Or you can listen to "The 'I' of My' Meditation" in the YouTube playlists, "Meditations from Awareness Explorers" or "Brian Tom O'Connor Meditations."

ੴ

This is not original to me. I simply put it into my own words. It's akin to the "self-inquiry" practice of the great twentieth century Indian sage Ramana Maharshi and his "who am I" question, as well as countless other wise folks since.

The idea, as in all awareness games, inquiry meditations, and imagination meditations, is to turn your attention around from "what you're looking at, to what's looking," as Loch Kelly puts it. What's looking is not any of the things listed above. These are objects, and are therefore seen by something else. But what's looking is not an object. What's looking is pure awareness, the background of all experience, the "I" of "my."

And this is where happiness, peace, and joy live. In the clear, choiceless, loving ground of being, which is already here, already accepting, just waiting to be noticed. Noticed by what? By itself. The unconditional love of pure awareness. In other words, by you.

Inquiry Meditation: Identity Shift
Be Awareness

This meditation is all about inquiring into your identity beyond your concepts of what you take to be yourself. It starts with the undefined identity of a newborn child and expands into an exploration of who or what is noticing your experience. It invites you to investigate the mystery of the self—the "I"—your true nature.

- First, as always, get comfortable, take an easy deep breath, and relax.
- See if you can notice any tension or holding or clutching in your body, and just let it be, as you breathe into it.
- Imagine you were just born a little while ago.
- Imagine you haven't learned any of the words or concepts or fears or ideas about yourself and the world that you've accumulated up to now.
- Imagine that none of the images about who you are and about what the world is like have formed yet. You know nothing of the world, or of yourself.
- Imagine looking out through the eyes of a newborn child with no name yet, no self-definition, no concept of a separation between you and everything else.
- It all just is. Here I am. I am here. It's all just appearing in me. My experience is me. I am my experience.
- Imagine that the "I" that's looking out through these newborn eyes continues to look out as I grow and learn things. Each new thing I learn is appearing to the same "I." The same clear background of awareness that I am.
- When I hear a word, or see an image, it appears in that clear background. But the background doesn't change with each new word or image.

- At five years old, it's the same clear background looking out through my eyes as when I was one. At ten years old, it's the same clear spacious awareness that I call "I" that was looking out through my eyes when I was five. At twenty, thirty, forty, it's the same clear spacious awareness that I call "I" that was looking out through my eyes when I was a little child.

- Now imagine you're the age you are right here, right now.

- Are you hearing sounds? Who's noticing that sound? You may answer "I am." But who is this "I"? What is this "me" that notices?

- Are you noticing thoughts flowing through your mind? Who's noticing those thoughts? "I am." Who is that "I"? What is this "me" that notices? Who is that voice in your head talking to?

- Are you noticing sensations in your body? Who's noticing that sensation? "I am." But who is this "I"? What is this "me" that notices?

- Do you have an image of your body? Who sees that image? Is it your body? Or something bigger? Who has a body?

- Do you have an idea of your personality? Who is aware of that idea? Is it your personality? Or something bigger that contains your personality? Who or what has a personality?

- If I'm not my body, or my thoughts, or my personality? Who or what am I?

- Remember the innocent, pure, clear awareness looking out of your eyes when you were just born. See if you can imagine, just for the duration of this little exploration, that who you are is that clear, empty, fresh, beautiful knowingness that includes your body, your thoughts, and your experience, but is bigger, more spacious than your body, your mind, or your personality.

- Let go of all concepts about yourself. Let go of all images of yourself. Let go of all borders or edges to yourself. That borderless infinite field is the universe looking at itself through your eyes. It's your true nature.

- You're not a concept, because all concepts appear in you. You're not a self-definition, because all self-definition appears in you. You're not your body, because your body appears in you.

- Be that in which everything appears.

- Be Awareness itself. I, awareness. I am. I.

NOTE: Since this is a long guided meditation, it might be useful to have someone read this slowly to you out loud. Or you could record it into your phone in your own voice and play it back. Or you can listen to the audio version of this book when it comes out. Or you can listen to "Identity Shift Meditation" in the YouTube playlists, "Meditations from Awareness Explorers" or "Brian Tom O'Connor Meditations."

Game Break: Your Name Here
A third person game

This is a great way to get a feel for not being your ego, your body, or your personality.

- In your thoughts, just for a few minutes, replace every instance of "I" with your name.

- For example, you might follow your thoughts in this manner:
"[Your name here] is thinking."
"[Your name here] is thinking about what to write."
"[Your name here] has a slight headache."
"Does [Your name here] want to have a little fruit right now?"
"[Your name here] went to the store yesterday to buy some fruit."
"[Your name here] wishes mangoes were in season."

I don't recommend talking out loud this way, at least not when other people are around. It's an unnecessary affectation, and most people will just think you're crazy. It also puts the focus on the interactions rather than on your true nature before your name.

But I do recommend trying the variation below every time you feel something you'd rather not feel, or think about yourself in a negative or judgmental way.

If you're feeling some emotion you don't want to be feeling, just say to yourself, "There goes [your name here] again, feeling [emotion you don't want]."

If you just got down on yourself for a habit or trait you don't like, just say to yourself, "There goes [your name here], doing that [habit you don't like] again."

If you just got down on yourself for a trait you don't like, just say to yourself, "There goes [your name here], being [trait you don't like] again."

Some examples:

- "There goes [your name here] again, feeling anxious."
- "There goes [your name here] again, feeling angry."
- "There goes [your name here] again, feeling sad."
- "There goes [your name here], being lazy again."
- "There goes [your name here], eating too much again."
- "There goes [your name here], letting his mind wander in meditation again."
- "There goes [your name here], being judgmental again."
- "There goes [your name here], being shy again."
- "There goes [your name here], being a jerk again."

Here's another variation:

The Name Game
Your name here again

Have you ever noticed that when you repeat a familiar word over and over in your mind, that it loses all meaning and just becomes an abstract sound?

The great poet Alfred Tennyson tried repeating his own name silently.

> "A kind of walking trance—this for lack of a better word—I have frequently had, quite up from boyhood, when I have been all alone. This has often come upon me through repeating my own name to myself silently till all at once, as it were, out of the intensity of the consciousness of individuality, the individuality itself seemed to resolve and fade away into boundless being, and this not a confused state, but the clearest of the clearest, the surest of the surest, utterly beyond words, where death was an almost laughable impossibility, the loss of personality (if so it were) seeming no extinction, but the only true life."

So try this:

- Repeat your name over and over again in your mind until it loses all meaning.
- Try it with just your first name, and then try your whole name.

Tennyson described this mystical experience in his poem, "The Ancient Sage."

> ...for more than once when I
> Sat all alone, revolving in myself
> The word that is the symbol of myself,
> The mortal limit of the Self was loosed,
> And passed into the nameless, as a cloud

Melts into heaven. I touch'd my limbs, the limbs
Were strange, not mine—and yet no shade of doubt,
But utter clearness, and thro' loss of Self
The gain of such large life as matched with ours
Were sun to spark—unshadowable in words,
Themselves but shadows of a shadow-world...

Tennyson said of his mystical experience, "By God Almighty! there is no delusion in the matter! It is no nebulous ecstasy, but a state of transcendent wonder, associated with absolute clearness of mind."

This took a while for me, as it might for you, but try it and persist. At first, "Brian" was me. So repeating the name seemed to point to myself. Eventually, "Brian" became a bundle of thoughts, sensations, memories, habits, preferences, and stories that are observed by something other than "Brian." That's when the "nebulous ecstasy" and "transcendent wonder" came into the picture. The nebulous ecstasy and transcendent wonder appeared to be what I truly am, and yet, at the same time they flooded back into Brian. Words are practically useless to adequately describe this, so don't go by my words, or Tennyson's, but play with it yourself.

Inquiry Meditation: The Dream Character
Life is but a dream?

- Recall a dream you've had. Any dream. The content doesn't matter. Any dream that you remember having.

- Recall the events in the dream and notice what was happening, and where it was happening—meaning the environment in which it was happening, and most importantly, who it was happening *to*.

- Who was the person experiencing the events in the dream, whether running away from something, or driving a car, or eating, or flying, or falling, or whatever?
  - Let's call the person having that dream "the dream character." In the dream of course, it feels like you. The dream happens to you. But often the dream character is not exactly the same as the you today. For example, it may be a younger you, or maybe a different person altogether.

- So imagine you are the dream character in the dream environment taking part in the dream events. Really visualize it in your imagination.

- Now imagine that you've woken up from the dream and you realize that you're not in that dream environment or involved in those dreamed events; you're lying in your bed in the present time with your present body at your present age.

- What happened to the dream character? Was the dream character real? Did the dream character wake up? What was the dream character made of?
  The dream character was made of the content of the dreamer's mind. That is, of your mind.

- Now imagine you're dreaming the exact experience you're having now. Perhaps you're sitting in a chair reading or listening to this book. Everything in the dream is exactly as it appears to you now, except you're dreaming.

- Now imagine that you wake up. Who has woken up? You? But you were the dream character. What was the dream made of? What were you—the dream character—made of?

- Imagine just for now that what has woken up was awareness. That what had experienced the dream was simply awareness. *It's awareness's dream.*

- Imagine that everything that happened in the dream— including you and all your experiences—happened in awareness's mind. It was made of awareness's mind. Which is to say, made of awareness.

- Now simply notice your present experience. Notice that it appears to be happening to you.

- But just for now, imagine that everything in your experience—the sights, the sounds, the body sensations, the other people, you yourself—everything is simply made of awareness.

- Awareness is dreaming you having this experience. Everything you experience is made of awareness's mind, which is to say of awareness itself.

- Now imagine you are pure awareness in which all experience appears, and you've just woken up from the dream of being a body in a room reading some words or listening to a voice.

There is another way of looking at the dream metaphor. Lucid dreaming is when we are asleep and dreaming, but during the dream we know that we are dreaming. This can also apply to universal awareness. In this case, it's universal awareness that is lucid dreaming it is an individual.

NOTE: Since this is a long guided meditation, it might be useful to have someone read this slowly to you out loud. Or you could record it into your phone in your own voice and play it back. Or you can listen to the audio version of this book when it comes out. Or you can listen to "Dream Meditation" in the YouTube playlists,

"Meditations from Awareness Explorers" or *"Brian Tom O'Connor Meditations."*

A Safety Precaution—Favorite Person

I had a question from a friend who was concerned that awareness practices could lead to a shift in identity in such a way that he would lose himself. And that was frightening to him. He went on to elaborate that he likes himself. He's comfortable with this personality—this ego that he is. He enjoys himself and he doesn't want that to go away. I totally sympathize with him. I wouldn't want my Brian-ness to go away either. I like Brian. He's a good guy. He enjoys himself a lot.

After mulling over this question for some time, it occurred to me that there's another way of thinking about all of this.

Do you have a favorite person, or a favorite character in a book, or a favorite artist, or a favorite writer, a favorite athlete, or some person that you really love, identify with, enjoy, know a lot about, follow, and who occupies a lot of your thought and emotion?

When your identity shifts from the ego personality to the larger Universal Consciousness in which you appear, you don't lose your personality or your ego identity, it just becomes like your favorite artist, or your favorite athlete, or your favorite fictional character. Someone you know about, someone you care about, someone you enjoy spending time with, someone you nurture, or simply someone you appreciate as part of your life. The "Little Me" is like that. It can be something that the "Big I" enjoys. It doesn't disappear. It doesn't go away. It doesn't have to be denied.

It can be enjoyed in all its humanness—in all its strengths, and flaws, and foibles, and preferences, and talents, and tastes.

The Big I can celebrate the Little Me.

Universality revels in particularity. That's why particularity exists in the first place—to be reveled in. So go revel!

෨

Some Final Thoughts About "I"

I've taken a lot of time in this section to elaborate on the shift in identity, because it's been the cornerstone of my practice for so many years. I started simply by silently repeating the word "I" and looking inside to see what that represents. At first my mind was very obliging and came up with lots of contenders, including my body, my personality, and my mind. ("To whom do thoughts appear?" "To other thoughts, of course," I would reply.)

But if I didn't settle for any of these (because, after all, who has a body? who has a personality? who has a mind?), and instead, kept returning to the *felt* sense of "I," then that indescribable, wordless, conceptless, vast, joyful all-inclusive sense of "I" would grow stronger and stronger. I discovered that it's absolutely reliable, since it never ever goes away. And the problems of the Little Me don't amount to a hill of beans in the Big I.

So feel free to simply stay with feeling of "I" and play with that.

THE WILD BLUE YONDER

Imagination is one of the most powerful forces in the universe. Possibly second only to unconditional love. Even physiologically, your whole system responds to something fully imagined as if it is really happening. This is the essence of method acting. It's also the essence of awareness practices. You don't actually have to believe that you are the entire universe looking out through your eyes in order to make direct contact with the infinite joy at the heart of all existence, you just have to imagine that you are—vividly, intensely. And when you do, the channel opens, and the love comes pouring through from the wild blue yonder into the earthly body that you temporarily occupy.

Here's a group of explorations and meditations that draw on your imagination. I imagine you'll have a favorite among them. Give them all a try and see.

Imagination Meditation: Be the Sky
Up we go

The object of this exploration is to imagine that you are the sky above the clouds, looking at whatever appears from the clear blue infinite space of pure awareness.

- Imagine that you're looking up at a clear blue sky. A pure beautiful cloudless blue sky stretching to infinity.

- Now imagine a little puffy white cloud wafts into view. Then another one. And then a bigger cloud. But plenty of blue sky can still be seen.

- And then some bigger, darker clouds appear. And more big dark clouds. And then the whole sky is filled with dark rain clouds. You can't see even a patch of blue anymore. Then it starts to rain. And thunder. And lightning.

- Where's the blue sky? Is it still there, behind the clouds and the rain?

Let's see.
- Let's start over. Clear all the clouds and rain, and start again with a clear blue sky.

- Imagine that you're looking up at a clear blue sky. A pure beautiful cloudless blue sky stretching to infinity.

- This time, imagine you're floating up into the sky. Up and up above the cloud level.

- Now turn around and look down and notice a little puffy white cloud wafting into view below you. Then another one. And then a bigger cloud. Around you and behind you, there's plenty of blue sky.

- And then some bigger, darker clouds appear. And more big dark clouds. The same big clouds that filled the whole sky when you were looking up at them, but now you're above them, floating in blueness, looking at the storm below.

- Rain. Thunder. Lightning. You're the blue sky watching the clouds and rain and lightning, but your blueness remains.
- Watch from above the clouds.
- Be the Sky. That's pure awareness.
- Now, still imagining yourself as the clear blue sky, watch as some thoughts roll through. Light fluffy thoughts at first, but then some darker ones. And then some emotions roll into view. Stormy feelings, with all the accompanying tension and internal argument and strategies to get rid of the feelings. Tears fall like rain.
- But you're the blue sky of awareness, above the storm level, calmly and serenely watching the torrent of thoughts and emotions, knowing that you're untouched by them. Knowing that your lovely pure blue self is unharmed, unconcerned, and will remain blue and serene after the stormy thoughts and emotions dissipate and roll away, as if they'd never been there at all.

You are the untouched, unharmable, serene, silent, spacious, clear sky of pure awareness.

NOTE: Since this is a long guided meditation, it might be useful to have someone read this slowly to you out loud. Or you could record it into your phone in your own voice and play it back. Or you can listen to the audio version of this book when it comes out.

Exploration: The Circle of This
How long can you stay in it?

This exploration has been highly effective for me as a present-moment happiness inducer.

The basic idea is that you create an image in your mind of "This," and draw a circle around it, then step inside the circle and see how long you can last without stepping out of it.

What do I mean by "this"? Everything that's happening right now, right here where you are. As in "Now. Here. This."

"This" means …
- o Whatever sights, sounds, feelings, and smells you're experiencing right now.
- o Whatever bodily sensation or emotions are showing up within you at this moment.
- o Whatever body image is appearing to you as it is, here and now.
- o Awareness of all of the above, meaning the "I" that's noticing whatever is appearing now and here.

"Not This" means…
- o Memories—scenarios of past events that run through your head like little movies in your mind.
- o Plans, fears, hopes for the future—little screenplays of how things are going to be at some future date and time.
- o Opinions about how things should or should not have been, or how they should or should not be in the future.
- o Imaginary conversations with people who are not here now.
- o Imaginary conversations with yourself.
- o Anything that draws your attention away from noticing what's happening right here, right now.

So here are the steps:
- • Sit comfortably.
- • Notice how your body feels right now.

- Notice any sounds that are happening now.

- Notice anything appearing to any of the five senses at the moment.

- Notice any inner sensations appearing right now.

- Draw a circle around all of this—your "circle of this."

- See if you can stay in the circle without stepping out into past memory or imagined future.

- If you do step out, just gently step back in again, and let whatever drew you out of the circle just float away.

- See how long you can stay with just "this."

Hint: Wordlessness helps. If you're having a verbal conversation in your head, even with yourself, you're probably out of the circle.

Another hint: Sounds and your body sensations are your friends and crewmates in this exploration—including your breathing. This is because sounds, breath, and body sensations are the most obvious elements of now, here, and this. And they can be experienced wordlessly.

This is why wordlessness is so useful. When you ask yourself, "What can I experience right now without using words to describe it or name it?" you are not fighting thought, or trying to stop thinking, you are turning your attention to something other than thought: to direct current experience of sensations and perceptions. It is a positive movement toward your current experience, and not a negative movement away from thinking.

When I play with The Circle of This, I fail pretty quickly. Thoughts of the past and future are insistent and seductive and continuously draw me away from present experience. That's okay. That's how it works. That's the challenge. After all, what if you played an arcade video game and there were no monsters or traps to avoid? But when I remember the tips above—wordlessness, sounds, and body sensations—I'm able to get back into the circle pretty easily. As long as I accept that I'll have to do this over and over, and stay wordless, the intrusions subside over time.

But what if I have one of those days when the intrusive thoughts don't subside? My most joyful discovery was that awareness does not leave when thoughts come in. I realized "Oh my gosh, I don't actually have to get rid of thoughts! Awareness is there all along, even when the thoughts keep coming." So, on those days when you can't quite seem to stay in the Circle of This, just notice that the awareness in which thoughts appear doesn't go away. It's always there and utterly reliable. So relax, go wordless, be awareness itself, and let thoughts come and go.

Exploration: What If?
Because imagination is enough

The opening phrase of this book is "What if?" which is also a recurring theme in *Awareness Games* as well as in *Awareness Adventures*. This is because imagination is one of the most powerful tools available for turning the mind towards the ground of being.

Play with these "what if's" for yourself:

- What if happiness wasn't something to get?
- What if happiness wasn't something that happened?
- What if happiness wasn't something that comes from outside or arrives from elsewhere? Or something you find in things, activities, achievements, people?
- What if happiness wasn't something to pursue, or to hope will happen sometime in the future?
- What if happiness was something that's already here? Inside each of us, just waiting, hoping to be noticed?
- What if happiness was our natural state, simply obscured by our thoughts about fixing, changing, improving? Obscured by the inherent unsatisfactoriness of our external lives?
- What if happiness was our true self, informed by the unconditional choiceless acceptance of all that is? This acceptance isn't something new that we need to do—it's something that awareness already does. All we have to do is notice it.

We don't become happy—we become happiness. Or better, we notice that we *already are* happiness.

The stuff to try in this book—the games, the adventures, the explorations that can be found here and in *Awareness Games* are ways to play around inside your mind to uncover the true self of happiness that is the background of all experience.

But because it's a little tricky, and because different things work at different time and for different people, I offer a variety of explorations, meditations, and games. We play with and experiment with awareness—we poke it, squeeze it, sniff it, bounce it—to see if we can stumble upon its true nature—and ours.

And when we discover the true nature of awareness, we discover that it's always present, always allowing, always open, always loving. We discover that it's always there. We don't have to create it or achieve it, but simply notice it.

When we notice that all of our experience appears in awareness, and we also notice that all of our experience appears to what we call "me," we realize that "me" and awareness are the same. And when we realize that all of that presence, allowing, openness, and love equals happiness, we see that we are happiness itself. We just to have notice it. Look past the dust and clouds of fixing, figuring out, improving, getting, achieving, and see that it's always there, and that it is us.

Game Break: Swimming Through Consciousness
Water—the other wild blue yonder

Turning from the sky to the ocean now, metaphorically, here's a game to get a sense that conscious awareness is all one substance. Just use your imagination and play with it.

- Notice whatever appears in consciousness, without trying to change any of it in any way.
  - Just let everything flow in and out of awareness, and flow freely from one thing to another, with no effort to control any of the natural flow.
- Imagine that it's all made of water, and you're swimming through it.
  - Sounds are made of water; thoughts are made of water; body sensations are made of water; emotions are made of water; sights are made of water; memories are made of water; images are made of water; imaginations are made of water; your body is made of water; everything else in the world is made of water; your sense of "I" is made of water; everything appearing in your mind is made of water.
- Swim through it all.
  - Swim through sounds; swim through thoughts; swim through body sensations; swim through emotions; swim through sights; swim through memories; swim through images; swim through imaginations; swim through your body is made of water; swim through everything else in the world; swim through everything appearing in your mind; swim through your sense of "I. " Swim through it all as if it is all made of water.
- It's all consciousness
  - Sounds are made of consciousness; thoughts are made of consciousness; body sensations are made of consciousness; emotions are made of consciousness;

sights are made of consciousness; memories are made of consciousness; images are made of consciousness; imaginations are made of consciousness; your body is made of consciousness; everything else in the world is made of consciousness; your sense of "I" is made of consciousness; everything appearing in your mind is made of consciousness.

- It's all one substance; one medium. But within that medium, different experiences take temporary form and then recede back into the one substance. All you have to do is to swim through each appearance as if you are a whirlpool of water just moving on through.

INTERNAL GEOGRAPHICAL SOCIETY

"While metaphors inevitably deform the experience ... they at least allow me to grasp hold of a shadow of it and, perhaps, share it."

~ Michael Pollan, *How to Change Your Mind*

All metaphors crash and burn eventually. Analogies too. Especially analogies. But this doesn't mean they're not useful until they do.

Why do they always crash and burn? Because they're made of words and words can't depict reality exactly. Reality is one thing. Not really a thing, but a thing-less thing. Just energy waving in different apparent forms. Nothing is separate from anything else except in appearance. There's only one thing: the universe making waves of form that rise and fall back into the infinite ocean of universal energy.

But words are thoughts. Words are concepts. Words are mind. The nature and purpose of words (and of concepts) is to distinguish things from one another. A useful tool to help an organism stay alive by deciding between what's food and what's poison, for instance. A useful tool for apparent organisms that want to stay organized as an entity. The mind is made of words and concepts, and as such, is the "organ of separation." But since there is only one thing going on, all separation is only apparent, and therefore words and concepts can never really describe ultimate reality.

What they *can* do is to point in the general direction of ultimate reality. However, if analyzed to a great degree, or taken literally, or put through the meat grinder of logic, they simply fall apart eventually.

However, the ultimate reality of oneness can flavor the mind. Or waft its perfume back towards the mind. We can get the sense of the unity of being through our own sense of being, our background awareness in which all things appear. Metaphors and analogies can help, at least until they crash and burn.

The classic metaphor about metaphors (you could call it a meta-metaphor) is the "finger pointing to the moon": A spiritual teaching is like a finger pointing to the moon, and should not be mistaken for the moon itself. Once your attention is directed toward the moon, there is no need to dwell on the finger.

The classic analogy that deals with the unique individual as part of the universal is "the wave and the ocean": Our individual bodies and minds are temporary forms, just like a wave is simply a temporary form that rises from the ocean, is never apart from ocean, is made of ocean, and falls back into ocean when the life of its form is over.

Which brings me to an analogy that occurred to me recently: The River Delta. It's often confusing how awareness can be universal, but we only know the content of our individual minds, not the content of other minds. How can both be true? Maybe this analogy will be helpful. It's sure to crash and burn under analysis, but I hope it's useful in the meantime. Here goes:

At the mouth of a river where the fresh river water empties into the salty ocean water, there is often a large area—a delta or an estuary where the river water meets the sea water. Imagine this is a large area with multiple streams and rivers from various sources all flowing into the ocean. In our analogy, the delta is our individual mind, and the ocean is the background of pure awareness. The delta only receives water from the rivers as they deposit sediment brought from upstream. It's a one-way stream. The water is flowing from upriver, through the delta, and out into the ocean. The delta doesn't receive water from the ocean flowing upstream.

The delta is like our individual mind. The content flowing from the outside world via our sense perceptions only flows one way—from the world, through our minds, and out into the ocean of awareness, leaving sediment in the form of memories. Our minds are only aware of the one-way flow of perceptions and sensations, and of the memories they deposit. But our thoughts and memories are witnessed by awareness itself, apart from our finite minds. This is the ocean of awareness that we all share.

Sometimes, as in an estuary, there is brackish water, a mixture of river water and sea water. So there's a taste of the sea present in the river mouth. A waft of sea breeze in the air. We can get that taste—that breeze of the ocean of awareness—when we take our focus off the one-way flow of our thoughts and drop back into the pure awareness that receives it all. We can create a two-way flow—between the delta of our individual minds, and the ocean of universal awareness. That's why meditative practices of quiet and stillness can invoke a sense of oneness. We're calming down the powerful rushing flow of sediment and letting some of the sea breeze waft in. And it feels absolutely lovely.

You can explore this for yourself. Try this:

Exploration: The River Delta
An estuarial adventure

- Imagine your mind as a river delta.
- The activities of the world are upstream.
- The awareness of the world is the ocean downstream.
- Your mind is the delta in between.
- Imagine the input from the world—the sights, sounds, sensations, smells, and tastes—as a one-way flow through your mind, flowing downriver into the vast awareness in which all thoughts, sensations, and perceptions appear.
- If it helps, imagine the streams and rivers flowing toward you from the front, and then flowing out to the sea of awareness behind you.
- As you imagine that flowing stream, see if you can imagine it calming down, and feel yourself gently, quietly floating down into the ocean of awareness that receives it all—the awareness that you are.
- And then imagine that the ocean of awareness, like the oceans of our earth, is connected to all the oceans. The one interconnected world ocean. It's an ocean of love because it knows it's all one ocean.
- Now imagine that the downstream flow of the river of thought quiets down just enough so that the ocean's saltiness can flavor the delta of your mind.

And if that metaphor crashes on the shoals for you, you can always go back to the simple "wave in the ocean" analogy.

More Metaphors

The TV Screen

Another terrific metaphor, from the great spiritual teacher Rupert Spira, is that of the TV screen. In this analogy, awareness is like the television screen, and the content of awareness is like the images that appear on it. According to Rupert, "If we identify our self as the screen we just remain as we are, allowing our self to take all these names and forms but without ever truly losing our identity to any of them." When we watch the screen, we may see a landscape and a person, but there is not actually a landscape or a person; all there is the screen. The landscape and the person are made of the screen, not separate from it or from each other.

In Rupert's analogy, awareness is like the screen, except that it's a self-aware screen, and the only thing that it actually experiences is itself. The landscape is made of awareness. The person is made of awareness. Neither one exists as a separate entity. The person in the landscape, however, doesn't know the screen; can't see the screen. Only the screen knows the screen, and therefore only the screen can wake up to its true nature, just as only awareness can wake up to its true nature as the knowing of all experience, or "the light of pure knowing," as Rupert calls it.

The Security Console

At one point, he expanded on this metaphor and introduced the analogy of the night watchman in a security station, a metaphor which I find even more satisfying. I'm paraphrasing, but the gist of it is this: Imagine a building with several security cameras throughout, both inside and out, each receiving images from a different room, area, and angle. Imagine the night watchman sitting at a desk looking at the security console, which contains a screen that shows the current image from each of the cameras. To the eye, the screen is made up of several separate squares, each with a different camera image, but if you run your finger along the screen, no division can be detected. It's all one screen. This is a great metaphor for individual consciousness, represented by the separate image captured by each camera, and universal consciousness, which is the security monitor, and contains all the images, but without separation.

Ah, but who's the night watchman? Look inside and see for yourself.

The Limitation Game

Consider the game of Monopoly. There is a two-dimensional board on which squares have been drawn separating them one from the other. By mutual agreement (the rules and our willingness to follow them when playing with each other), we go along with the fiction that these squares represent real estate divisions, some of which are owned by one player and some of which are owned by others. In addition, we mutually agree that our movement among these imaginary pieces of real estate is constrained by the random roll of a pair of dice. We also agree that little colored pieces of paper define our ability to buy, sell, and improve our fictional real estate properties. Finally, we agree that our movement is dictated by the order in which we sit around the board.

In other words, we voluntarily allow limitations to be imposed where none exist. Limitations on ownership, limitations on mobility, limitations on resources, and limitations on our freedom of action.

However, in reality, these limitations don't exist! The real estate divisions are simply colored ink on cardboard. We have the physical freedom to move our little tokens anywhere around the board—or anywhere else in the room—that we please. Our buying power is just bits of colored paper with numbers printed on them. We can get up and walk around the room any time we please. When we go to the kitchen to get a beer, the limitations of the Monopoly board don't apply.

If we apply this metaphor in the spirit of playfulness appropriate to its nature as a game, we can use it to gain insight into the nature of absolute reality.

All reality is simply energy temporarily appearing as different forms. It appears that we are limited to our physical bodies and all other people and animals are limited to theirs. But when we imagine that all experience appears in the one unified field of awareness, and that in fact, no experience (including objects of perception) can appear outside of awareness, we realize that all experience is made of awareness. And awareness is one indivisible unlimited field. So all the apparent limitations that we see and sense in the physical world have no more reality than the mutually agreed upon rules of a Monopoly game.

As always, you don't need to believe any of this is true, you simply have to play with the idea. That's enough to point your mind in the direction of the unlimited field of awareness.

The Water Bottle

What if someone told you about a very special and rare group of people who never had to drink water? These gifted and advanced individuals had achieved a special state in which they never got thirsty, never became dehydrated, and therefore never had to drink water for the rest of their lives. You were also told it took many years of esoteric training to achieve this marvelous state.

Let's say you were so intrigued by this that you felt you had to try to join their advanced ranks and become a non-water-drinker yourself. You tried the secret practices for many years but no luck— you were still thirsty all the time.

Now imagine you were told that there was an easier way. You could make sure you always carried a water bottle with you, and you could drink from it any time you felt thirsty. And what if you also learned two things about a special type of water bottle: One, that it's never empty—It's infinitely refillable, and two, that you already had one with you, and you will always have one with you no matter where you go or what you do.

You now have two choices: You could continue the esoteric practices to achieve non-water-drinker status, because you feel that only those who have worked hard and disciplined themselves are deserving enough to not be thirsty all the time. Or you could trust your infinitely refillable ever-present water bottle that's always with you.

Which route would you choose?

The infinitely refillable bottle is, of course, the pure background of awareness that you are, but don't usually notice. You don't have to achieve a state of "permanent awareness." You just have to notice (or simply imagine) that you are never *not* aware, and that you actually *are* awareness itself, not the body and mind and personality you take yourself to be. This infinitely refillable bottle of joy is always there, and when you see it as you, you realize you can never leave it behind, for how can you walk away from yourself?

It's the connection between your individual mind and the universal mind. And once you get the hang of drinking from it at will—voila! You can stop trying to become the sort of super-human person who is permanently enlightened and never has to drink.

And not only can you give up the idea of becoming the sort of person who never has to drink, you can give up the idea that in order to stay hydrated, you have to be drinking from the bottle constantly, 24/7. It's simply there whenever you want it or need it. You can go about your life, hydrated and worry-free, and simply drink when you're thirsty.

※

Awareness itself is like the infinitely refillable water bottle. It's an infinite well of joy. It's the clear unconditioned field within you that notices all of your experience—that witnesses all of your experience. When you connect to the witnessing or noticing field within, and allow this moment to be exactly as it is, joy and bliss bubble up in the heart.

And you can connect to it in three simple steps:

- First, just for now, accept everything in your present experience to be exactly as it is.

- Second, shift your attention from the content of awareness to awareness itself—that which knows all of your experience.

- Third, turn around again and look at the world from that knowingness which is the real you.

And for extra credit...

- See the world you're looking at—which indeed, appears in you, awareness—as none other than yourself. You, looking at yourself. Awareness being aware of awareness. The universe seeing itself through your eyes.

And the universe is totally happy with itself.

Exploration: Maps Without Borders
Imaginary lines

There's a spot in the United States called the four corners. It's where the southwest corner of Colorado, the southeast corner of Utah, the northeast corner of Arizona, and the northwest corner of New Mexico all meet. This is possible because each of these states have at least two adjacent borders that are straight lines, that is, not created by any geographical feature like a river or a seashore. Each pair of straight lines forms a right angle, and four of these right angles touch each other at one spot.

Tourists enjoy standing on the Four Corners monument with one foot in one state and one foot in another state. Maybe even putting one hand down in a third state and the other hand in the fourth state. Are their four limbs actually touching anything that's different from each other in any real sense? If you step across the border from Colorado, say, to New Mexico, have you stepped over anything real? Is there a physical line in the dirt or a change of soil that tells you you've stepped from one state to another? No. The lines are simply mutually agreed upon imaginary lines that demark political jurisdiction.

- Imagine awareness is like this. (Just imagine it—it's not necessary to believe it's true.)
- Imagine that everything you experience, that is, everything that you're aware of, appears simultaneously in the same awareness.
- Imagine the sounds you hear are Colorado, sights are Utah, smells are New Mexico, and thoughts are Arizona.
- Notice that they all appear in one field of awareness.
- Notice that awareness is undivided.
- Enjoy the U.S.A.—the United States of Awareness

Pixels

A similar analogy: pixels on a TV screen or computer monitor. Imagine a screen with a white background and a red dot that moves across the screen from left to right. Is there something real that exists and moves across the screen? Or is there simply this?: Pixel #1 on the left side turns from white to red, and then, as it turns back to white again, pixel #2 to its immediate right turns red. Then pixel #2 turns white again as pixel #3 turns red, and so on.

We perceive it as a red dot travelling across a white field. But that's an illusion. There is no dot separate from the background; there is just a screen with little areas that change the vibration of light that they emit. There is no border or boundary between the red dot and the white field, since there is no red dot. It's just the screen's light energy fluctuating in a way that our minds perceive as a pattern.

What if the universe and all that you experience was like that? What if what we perceive as separate objects, places, and people are simply small areas of the one field temporarily changing its properties?

Imagining that everything in the world is simply one single field of energy can lead us to envisioning that there is no real distinction between one thing and anything else. We can sense that all the inner borders we picture in our minds and feel in our emotions are simply imaginary.

So let's go even further and play with dissolving these borders.

Meditation: Dissolving Borders

- Close your eyes and take a few easy deep breaths.
- Dissolve all borders between anything and everything:
    - Look inside at your thoughts, your perceptions, and your sensations, and notice all the borders, barriers, and distinctions between things that your mind entertains.
    - And for each border or distinction that you notice, simply imagine it dissolving into nothing as you breathe.
    - These borders and barriers include any thoughts that people should be different than they are. Notice them and dissolve them.
- My hand is separate from my arm. That's a border that's only in my mind.
- My body is separate from the chair. That's a border that's only in my mind.
- The door is separate from the hall. That's a border that's only in my mind.
- I am separate from the air that I breath. That's a border that's only in my mind.
- I am separate from you. That's a border that's only in my mind.
- Notice and dissolve all borders that pop into awareness.
- Notice and dissolve any definition of yourself.
- Notice and dissolve any borders between yourself and the world.
- Notice and dissolve all compartments that keep certain types of things separate from other types of things.
    - These can be mental compartments that separate thoughts and feelings from each other; that separate body sensations from sounds; that separate all sensations from perceptions.

- Dissolve all borders between one part of your body and another. Go inside and notice the walls in your mind that separate parts of you from other parts, and imagine them dissolving.

- Dissolve all borders between you and the air around you. Imagine the border of your skin becoming so porous you can breathe through it, and then eventually dissolving completely.

- Notice any resistance to the way other people speak and behave, and notice that this resistance is an internal barrier. It's only in your mind, and you can dissolve it.

- Notice any resistance to events or situations in your life, and notice that this resistance is an internal barrier. It's only in your mind, and you can dissolve it.

- Simply sit quietly and wait for inner borders, and walls, and barriers, and resistances to rise into awareness, and as they do, simply imagine them dissolving as you breathe.

- After a while, you don't even have to attach words to the inner borders you notice. You don't even have to envision them clearly and distinctly. Some inner borders are simply felt inside without words or pictures.

- Just sit and imagine all inner and outer borders dissolving.

Game Break: Pick-Up Sticks
Removing the boundaries in your mind

This is the same as the guided meditation above, but in a shorter, gamified version.

- Look in your mind for any borders or boundaries between anything and anything else. You can look at them as lines, or as sticks like in pick-up sticks, or as Jenga blocks.
- Simply look for them, and when you find them, remove them one by one.
  - It's easy to recognize the boundary lines: anything you don't like, any person you don't agree with, any emotion you don't want to feel, any distinction between one thing and another thing, any opinion about anything, any sense of inside and outside, or myself and other.
- When you remove each border line, imagine it like you were removing a wall separating two areas of color like blue and yellow. When you remove the wall, the two areas blend into one green area.
- Get creative. Be a detective. The more you play, the subtler the borders you find will be.

Sometimes there can be a chain reaction. Removing one boundary line causes a whole bunch of others to fall away. In fact, the only difference between this game and pick-up sticks or Jenga blocks is that when the whole structure comes tumbling down, you win.

Even More Metaphors for Awareness

Blank paper

Awareness is like the blank paper upon which words are written. Shifting your attention from the words to the blank paper is just like shifting your attention from the content of awareness to awareness itself. This also works well with a blank whiteboard.

Silence

Similarly, imagine that sounds appear in silence. In other words, silence is the empty field in which sounds appear. It's already there before the sounds are heard. Like a concert hall before a concert. The silence is there before the sound of the concert. You wouldn't be able to hear the sound were it not for the silence in which it appears.

Spaciousness

This is another "container" metaphor for pure awareness. It's useful to imagine that all things appear in spaciousness. Including yourself. Of course, as with all metaphors, this breaks down after a while because ultimately, spaciousness is not separate from that which appears in spaciousness. All that appears is made of spaciousness, or awareness itself. But it helps to make this a two-step process: first imagine spaciousness separately from its content, then imagine that all that appears is made of spaciousness.

Construction Site

Here's another metaphor for universal consciousness: Imagine a construction site with plywood walls separating the site from the sidewalks around it. Imagine those little square windows through which passers-by can peek in at the workers and the progress they're making.

Each little square affords a view at a slightly different angle from the other squares. These windows are like our individual minds, each viewing the world from a slightly different vantage point. Universal consciousness, or awareness, can not only look through any window it chooses, but can look through all the windows at the same time.

Of course, this metaphor is incomplete, although useful. For the analogy to be complete, we'd have to imagine that the viewer is not only outside the construction site, but inside it, completely surrounding it, and ultimately not separate from the wall, the windows, or the site itself. This is hard to imagine with our limited minds, however, so use this as a training-wheel metaphor to get you going. For a more advanced version, see "Mission Control," below.

Meditation: Quadrangulation
Sounds plus Sensations plus Visual Field plus Thoughts

This meditation builds upon the earlier one, "Triangulation," by adding a fourth element—your visual field.

Because visual content with eyes open is so distracting and seems to actively pull our attention outward towards objects that are supposedly "out there," I recommend experiencing the visual field with your eyes closed. Just notice the abstract colors and shapes that appear behind your eyelids. After you master this meditation, feel free to try the visual field steps with your eyes open, but if you do, try to see objects without naming them or creating mental verbal descriptions of them. In other words, still see them as abstract colors, shapes, and patterns.

As with the Triangulation meditation, we are experiencing the all-inclusiveness of awareness by noticing that more than one mode of experience appears in the same field of awareness at the same time.

If you haven't tried the Triangulation meditation, I recommend you try that first, and when you get a good intuitive feel of it, move on to this one.

Here's the Quadrangulation meditation:

- Starting with your eyes closed, listen to the sounds around you—the hum of an air conditioner or heater, or perhaps the sounds of traffic or birds or wind outside, or the sound of my voice.
  - As you notice the sounds that appear, ask yourself, "What is the silent field in which the sounds appear?"
  - Notice each sound separately, and ask the question, "What is the silent field in which this sound appears?"
  - Now see if you can notice all the sounds at the same time, and ask yourself, "Do all the sounds appear in the same silent field?"

- Then notice your bodily sensations—the feel of your body on the chair, or your feet on the floor. Perhaps a breeze on your skin, or the rise and fall of your belly as you breathe.
  - As you notice the sensations that appear, ask yourself, "What is the empty spacious field in which sensations appear?"
  - Notice each sensation separately, and ask the question, "What is the empty spacious field in which this sensation appears?"
  - Now see if you can notice all the sensations at the same time, and ask yourself, "Do all these sensations appear in the same empty spacious field?"
- Now see if you can notice both sounds and body sensations at the same time.
  - Ask yourself, "Is the field in which sounds appear, the same as the field in which sensations appear?" This is the clear field of awareness.
- Notice what thoughts are appearing now.
  - Imagine the thoughts are coming from somewhere outside of you and are projected on a blank screen inside you.
  - Imagine that the screen has both sound and subtitles, so you can either hear or read each thought that appears.
  - Imagine this screen is like a clear empty field in which thoughts appear.
  - As you notice the thoughts that appear, ask yourself, "what is the blank empty field in which these thoughts appear?"
  - Notice a few thoughts separately, as they appear in a sequence of thoughts, and for each one, ask yourself, "Do all these thoughts appear in the same empty field?"
- Now see if you can notice both the thoughts and the body sensation at the same time.

- o Ask yourself, "Is the field in which thoughts appear, the same as the field in which sensations appear?"
- Then see if you can notice both the thoughts and the sounds at the same time.
  - o Ask yourself, "Is the field in which thoughts appear, the same as the field in which sounds appear?"
    - ▪ Now see if you can notice all three—the sounds, the sensations, and the thoughts—appearing at the same time, and ask yourself, "Are these all appearing in the same clear empty field of awareness?"
- Keeping your eyes closed, notice what colors or patterns or shapes are appearing behind your eyelids. This is your visual field, which is still present even if your eyes are closed.
  - o As you notice the visual field and the colors and shapes that appear, ask yourself, "what is the blank empty field in which these colors and shapes appear?"
- Now see if you can notice both the visual images and the body sensation at the same time.
  - o Ask yourself, "Is the field in which visual images appear, the same as the field in which sensations appear?"
- Now see if you can notice both the visual images and the sounds at the same time.
  - o Ask yourself, "Is the field in which visual images appear, the same as the field in which sounds appear?"
- Then see if you can notice both the visual images and thoughts at the same time.
  - o Ask yourself, "Is the field in which visual images appear, the same as the field in which thoughts appear?"
    - ▪ Now see if you can notice all four—the sounds, the sensations, the thoughts, and the visual images—appearing at the same time, and ask yourself, "Are these all appearing in the same clear empty field of awareness?"

- Notice that in the open field of awareness, there are no borders or boundaries among any of these. No borders between thoughts, images, sounds, or sensations. They are all simultaneously appearing in one indivisible field of awareness.

- That field is your true nature. Clear, spacious, silent, allowing,

- Be that field. It's who you really are, so you might as well be that knowingly.

- Now, if your eyes are closed, gently open them again and take another easy breath.

NOTE: Since this is a long guided meditation, it might be useful to have someone read this slowly to you out loud. Or you could record it into your phone in your own voice and play it back. Or you can listen to the audio version of this book when it comes out.

FOUND IN SPACE

Mission Control

A common question is, "How can I be Universal Awareness if I can only see out of my own eyes, and I am only aware of my own thoughts?" Sometimes it's put another way: "How can awareness be infinite, can have no limits, when it seems that my awareness is limited to my individual thoughts and my individual field of perception? After all, I can't see what's on the other side of this wall, and I can't know another person's thoughts."

A good answer is that you are not your individual mind. Or, to put it another way, it is not your awareness that knows your individual mind.

It seems as if you have an individual awareness behind your eyes looking out, but that's the central illusion. You are not an individual awareness looking out, you are Universal Awareness, aware of the individual mind, which is really just a way station that filters the images as they travel from your eyes to awareness.

A good metaphor to help explain this is the robocam. Or if you prefer, a lunar module or a Mars rover. A Mars rover or a robocam is robot with a camera installed. The camera views its environment and sends that information back into the motion generator of the robot which uses that information to steer itself, to go around obstacles or to go toward a destination. A Mars rover also collects data from its cameras and other sensors. All this is programmed into the robocam or the Mars rover. However, the information that is coming in through the camera and through other sensors in the rover is not actually known by the rover, but is being transmitted to Mission Control.

You are not the rover; you are Mission Control.

Your body and your individual mind are the Mars rover, but you are Mission Control.

The Rover makes decisions about directions to move and actions to take based on the data it receives through its cameras, sensors from the environment it moves in, and, based on its programming and algorithms, its onboard computer. But it's not self-aware. There is no "self" in the rover. As John Wheeler puts it, "There's no such entity in the machine." The entity that's aware of the data it gathers, the information it receives, the actions it takes, and the pictures it records, is Mission Control.

Now of course, this metaphor only brings us halfway there, because Mission Control, if it is to represent awareness, would have to actually be everything that exists, because everything is a localization of universal awareness. And of course, Mission Control is something filled with particular qualities—people, instruments, technology, screens, rooms, machines, etc., whereas pure awareness has no qualities because anything that has a quality is something that could be described and named and therefore appears in awareness.

But we can put that aside for later, because this metaphor helps us take the first important step, which is to shift your identity from the individual body and the individual mind to the larger awareness in which the individual mind and the individual body appear. And you can think of this as Mission Control.

Your individual mind is limited to what can enter through the sense organs, or, in the case of a robot, through sensors or measuring devices. This information can be used by the robot to make decisions on what to do or where to move. However, it is Mission Control that knows this information—that is receiving this information—that is aware of this information and is aware of all the information sent by all the Mars rovers. (Let's assume there's a fleet of them.)

Once we've gotten a feel for it, we can extend this metaphor in a very useful way when we see that for us, our individual minds are actually porous—if we allow them to be. That is, if we can become quiet enough to allow information to flow in two directions: not only from the input of our sensory organs to awareness, but also from Universal Awareness to the individual mind, which is how intuition happens, and which is how extrasensory perception happens, and which is a how psychic knowing happens.

This is also how happiness happens. The second stream in the two-way flow from Universal Awareness to the individual mind is not simply information, but it's actually the feeling of universal love that comes from the total allowing nature of awareness itself. This is sometimes referred to as the perfume of consciousness that wafts from the universal into the individual. So it's not really information like a thought is information, it's more like a knowing that we can sense—a knowing that our true nature is this Universal Consciousness, which is clear, empty, allowing, loving. And this is happiness.

And to return to the metaphor, we can train ourselves to listen to mission control, to create a two-way data stream between the rover and Mission Control. But Mission Control—that is, Universal Consciousness—doesn't speak in the same language as the Mars rover—that is, our individual minds. It speaks nonverbally, non-conceptually, in a language that can only be sensed, not analyzed, or broken down into yes/no, good/bad concepts.

The Mission Control of Universal Consciousness is happier than the Mars rover of the individual body/mind, but when the two-way data stream is established, Mission control can start to transmit its happiness and well-being to the rover. The individual body, mind, and personality can actually feel the love and joy inherent in Universal Consciousness.

Even Further (Utterly Not Two)

This Mission Control metaphor is remarkably useful to help us identify with the larger universal consciousness, as opposed to the individual body and mind, which is simply a conduit for signals and programmed behavior. But even this doesn't go far enough, because in this metaphor, mission control and the rover are separate. Universal Consciousness and the individual are separate. It's a crucial first step, however, and absolutely necessary to see and feel that that the "you" that knows experience is not the individual "you" that you think of when you say your name, but the "you" as the universal receiving and knowing input from the individual.

The next step, however, is to see that these are really not two separate things.

Exploration: One Thing Going On
Just energy, waving

Try this (and you don't have to believe any of this is true, you simply have to imagine it is, just for now):

- Imagine that there is only one thing going on.
- Just energy.
- Just energy waving in different shapes and textures and colors, but just one field of energy.
- All of these temporary shapes and forms are made of the same single energy field and are not separate from each other.
- If one temporary form were to look at another temporary form, it would be seeing itself—the one energy field.
- Like two fingers rubbing together are part of the same hand. We conceptualize it as one finger feeling another, but it's the hand feeling itself.
- If all is one, and all is connected, and shape and form are simply temporary waves in the one ocean, then when I look at the world, aren't I seeing myself?
- When I look at others, aren't I seeing myself?

You may ask, "Yes, but why don't I know what's in other people's minds? Why don't I see what they see when they're somewhere else? Why can't I see through this wall?"

If so, you ask because you, the individual body and mind, are confusing the individual body and mind with the real you—the one that is simultaneously knowing the thoughts and sensations and perceptions of all bodies and all minds. You're not the Mars rover, you're Mission Control, but in our extended version of the metaphor, the rover is not separate, but simply an extension of Mission Control, utterly connected, utterly not two.

Like your fingers are part of your hand, and your hand is part of your body, and your body is part of humanity, and humanity is part of the animal kingdom, and the animal kingdom is part of life on earth, and life on earth is part of the planet, and the planet is part of the solar system, and, well, you get the idea. The separate nature of all these things is simply a concept—one that's useful, to be sure, in order to keep the temporary forms a little less temporary—but only a concept just the same.

And even further... What is this one thing that is the only thing going on? What is the one irreducible element of all experience, without which there would be no experience? Awareness.

Exploration: Awareness is All
And you are that

Try this (and you don't have to believe any of this is true, you simply have to imagine it is, just for now):

- Have you ever experienced anything without awareness?
- Have you ever actually experienced not being aware?
  (I'm not talking about remembering a time when you didn't notice you were aware, I'm talking about directly, presently, experiencing not being aware.)
- When you touch things, the feeling is happening in awareness.
- When you hear things, the sound is happening in awareness.
- When you see things, the sight is happening in awareness.
- When you touch things, the feeling is made of awareness.
- When you hear things, the sound is made of awareness.
- When you see things, the sight is made of awareness.
- What if all things are pervaded by awareness?
- What if nothing is separate from awareness?
- What if awareness is all there is?
- Wouldn't that mean you are awareness?
- Wouldn't that mean everyone and all things are awareness?

Now...

- What is this awareness like?
- Are there edges, or is it infinite? Imagine it's infinite.
- Did it stop and start, or has it always been present? Imagine it's eternal.
- What if awareness is infinite and eternal?
- Could there be more than one?
- What if there was only one? Who could you possibly be, other than infinite eternal awareness?

As I've mentioned over and over, you don't have to believe any of this is true. You simply have to play with it in your imagination, and you will be taking yourself to the place of infinite joy—your true nature. It's very tempting to raise logical objections to all of this. I know, I did it. I was the king of logical objections. But logic is not what helps you to experience the love, peace, and happiness at the heart of existence. What helps is to feel your way into it through playing with your imagination, looking inside, and looking out again from the space of awareness.

So...

You are not the Mars rover, you're Mission Control...

But...

Mission control and the Mars rover are not separate. All is Mission Control.

This is the central paradox of nonduality that many people miss: Duality exists within nonduality. You have to see what you're not before you can see that you're everything. I know it makes no sense to the mind. But you can feel your way into it. That's the great adventure.

Exploration: The Outer Limits
Does awareness even HAVE limits?

- Imagine this: you are sitting in the front seat of a car, stopped at an intersection, looking down a long straight street that extends for many blocks ahead of you.

- You see many buildings, trees, other cars, more traffic lights, and pedestrians along the street ahead. Maybe the street ends at a river and you can see across it into the distant landscape.

- The images of all those buildings, trees, cars, lights, and of the distant river and the landscape beyond all appear in awareness.

- Now imagine a long truck crosses the intersection, and stops in front of you, between you and the continuation of your street ahead.

- Ask yourself, "Did awareness just shrink, now that I can no longer see into the distance across the intersection? When the truck pulls away, does awareness expand again to include the street, buildings, lights, river, and landscape?

- Or is awareness limitless, borderless, infinite, able to include anything and everything that appears?

If you're playing with this at home, great. If you're in a car and you're a passenger, great. If you're driving, make sure you're stopped, and best not to close your eyes while you're imagining.

This exploration came out of an argument I was having with myself. Actually, an argument I was having with Rupert Spira, but only in my head. He would often ask, "Does awareness have any limits?" and I found that my mind wanted to resist going where he was leading. "Yes, it has limits," I would think, "It's limited by what I can take in through my senses." In other words, I can't see the other side of that wall, so therefore awareness is limited to what's on this side of the wall.

It took me a long time to come up with a satisfactory response to myself, but gradually I came to see that awareness is infinitely malleable, infinitely expandable, and able to contain anything and everything that the senses can send its way. The metaphor above is my attempt to give a picture of this new understanding.

Doing or Not Doing

There are many arguments in non-dual circles about whether achieving non-dual awareness or realizing your true nature involves actively doing something or not. And after contemplating this for quite a while, I realize there are many answers. For example, Rupert Spira's summary of how to practice his teaching is, "Be knowingly the presence of awareness." On the other hand, many nondualists say, "there is no you to do anything, so there is nothing to be done." Some find this helpful; some find it less so.

But I think the best metaphor for how to do non doing is relaxation.

Let's say your fists are clenched, and I asked you to unclench your fists. What do you do? You relax your hands and fingers. Is that doing or not doing? You could say relaxing is a doing of something. Or you could say relaxing is not doing, in the sense that you simply stop clenching.

If you have tension in your jaw and I say to you, relax your jaw. Just let it drop and hang open with no tension whatsoever. How do you do this? Is this a doing or not doing? You could say it's a doing of the act of relaxing. Or you could say it's a not doing in that you are no longer tensing your jaw muscles.

Non-dual awareness of awareness is the same thing. It's a doing, in that you are turning your attention from the content of awareness to awareness itself, but it's a non-doing in the sense that you're noticing something that is already there, not something you are bringing into being. In addition, you are dropping all of your strategies to bring something into being—or indeed to make what's arising in this moment any different from the way it is right now.

The doing that you are stopping doing is comprised of all of these strategies. For instance, figuring out what to say to someone to convince them you are right, tensing your muscles, trying to make the unwanted emotion go away by meditating or quieting the mind, promising yourself that you'll be different in the future, remembering the past, imagining the future, and many more.

These are like clenching your fists. To unclench your fists, you simply stop clenching. That's the non-doing I'm referring to.

Let's try it. Right now, let go of all tension in your jaw and just let it hang open in a fully relaxed way. Scan your body from the top of your head to your toes and see if there's any tension or clutching. If there is, just ask yourself, "Can I let go of this tension or clutching?" And take a breath.

Now notice your experience, including your thoughts and your body sensations, and ask yourself, "Is there any sense that I would like my current experience to be different than the way it is right now? Are there any strategies I'm using to fix myself, the world, or my current experience?" And simply drop the strategies.

It's doing something in that the act of dropping could be considered doing something, but it's really ceasing to do something. You're stopping the activity of trying to change your experience. Just like you're ceasing the activity of tensing your muscles in the act of relaxation.

Another thing you can drop, or stop doing, is describing your experience with words in your mind. To simply experience whatever you are experiencing right now without describing it with words in your mind is not-doing of the highest order. It is experiencing reality as it is, and not as filtered by conditioning, opinions, self-images, the past, or the future.

So, the way to do not doing is simply to relax all efforts to change anything or to describe anything. Is that doing or non-doing? I will leave it up to your mind to decide.

But I'll also remind you that you are not your mind. Your mind appears in you, awareness. And awareness is always there, effortlessly, and you don't have to do anything for it to be there, other than to simply notice it. In fact, you couldn't not be aware, even if you tried. You can't make awareness appear. You can't become more aware. You can only notice that awareness is already present, already allowing all that appears to appear, and already your natural state. It's the "I" behind all experience. All you have to do is notice it. And once you notice it, simply be it. Is that doing or non-doing? Who knows?

❧

One of the best metaphors I've found for the doing vs. non-doing / effort vs no-effort dilemma is this, from David R. Hawkins:

> Spiritual evolution is almost like a spaceship taking off from earth's gravity. It is difficult at first, but finally leaves the gravitational field. Energy consuming intentionality eventually dissolves into effortless surrender, and one becomes the recipient of unfolding awareness. Revelation replaces discovery. Understanding presents itself and becomes self-revealing by grace. Without effort, the inner pressure to achieve spiritual awareness is replaced by being the witness of truth, rather than its seeker. Effort is replaced by the effortlessness of spontaneous discovery. Essence progressively shines forth through form, which loses its delineation. Then, even essence fades into the domain of the awareness of existence itself, with its self-revealing divinity.[i]

So, there may be a little effort required to leave the mind's gravity. It's the least amount of effort possible to keep your attention on awareness itself and notice it's your true self.

FANTASTIC VOYAGE

Many spiritual and religious systems give the body short shrift. They either demonize it, ignore it, or deny its existence. The body is dirty or shameful; the body must be transcended; you are not your body. Well, the last one may be true—if you have a body, who's the you that has it? But your body is such a useful gateway into the infinite field of happiness, that it would be a shame to ignore it. Since we have to start with what's in awareness, and then walk back to awareness itself, the body is the perfect place to start. Use it!

•

Exploration: Into the Body
Feel your body from the inside

- Get comfortable, relax, and take a couple of slow easy deep breaths.

- Gradually turn your attention from the outside world to your inner world.

- Notice what's happening inside you. Your thoughts, your feelings, your sensations.

- Turn your attention from your thoughts and your emotions to your actual physical sensations—to the inner sense of your body. Feel your body from the inside.

- Notice any contractions or tensions you may be experiencing. Just notice them. No need to do anything about them, at least for now.

- Scan your body from the inside, from head to toe and see if you can notice whatever sensations and experiences you're having, without labeling them with words in the mind. Just notice pure sensation.

- Perhaps there is a tingling in your hands or legs or elsewhere. Perhaps there is a feeling of pressure or weight against the chair or floor.

- Visualize any and all of these sensations as abstract wordless patterns of experience, like a field of dots or vibrations.

- Notice the field of awareness in which all of these patterns of sensation appear.

- Be that awareness.

Game Break: Being Aware *FROM* the Place You Are Aware *OF*
Is awareness only in one place?

This game was inspired by Loch Kelly and his audiobook, *Effortless Mindfulness Now*ii.

If we look to find a self-center from which we are aware of all things, we don't find it. There isn't some part of our body, or our heads, or our brains, or our minds, or our thoughts that can be known as a center of self—something that comprises a self, looking at everything else. There simply isn't one. We can try as hard as we can to look for it, but we don't find it. And yet we feel that we are aware. We feel that we *are,* that is, that we exist, and we feel that we are aware.

So this game plays with the idea that, instead of being aware from some self-center, we are actually aware *from* the same place in which the thing we are aware *of* is located.

- Notice that you're aware of your hand. If there's no self-center to be aware from, the awareness of your hand must be in your hand.

- Notice that you're aware of your face. If there's no self-center from which to be aware, then you must be aware in your face. Awareness exists in that place, and you're aware from that place.

- Bring your attention to your right knee. Notice that, if you're aware of your right knee, and there's no self-center to be aware from, then you're aware *in* your right knee, *from* your right knee.

- Bring your attention to the heart area in the center of your chest. Sense that awareness exists in your heart center, and that you can be aware *from* your heart center.

- Bring your attention to your entire body. If there's no self-center to be aware from, then you're aware from your entire body

- So, we've found that we're aware from our hand; we're aware from our face; we're aware from our right knee; we're aware from our heart center; we're aware from our entire body. What does this mean?
    o Could it mean that our hand, our face, our knee, our heart, and our entire body are all part of awareness, indeed are made of awareness?
- And if this is true, what if we're aware of a table in the room that we're looking at? Are we aware from the table? I say yes.
- Look out the window. Are you aware from the tree, from the street, from the sky that you're looking at? I say yes.
- Which makes the table, the window, the tree, the street, and the sky part of awareness and indeed made of awareness.

At the risk of repetition, I'll remind you once again that you don't have to *believe* that your knee, a table, or a tree are made of awareness. You just have to *play with it*. It's the asking if it's possible, and the looking for yourself, that is the real practice, the real exploration, not the answer you may or may not come up with.

Game Break: What is Aware of Your Body?
Are you your Body? If you think so, try this.

The simplest way to overcome the "I am the body" idea is to ask yourself one of these questions:

- "What is aware of my body?"

Or

- "What notices my body?"

Or

- "What does my body appear in?"

Or

- "What experiences my body?"

In each case, whatever it is, it's not your body.

- Be that.

❧

The whole thing about the body is one of the great paradoxes. We seem to be separate bodies, and yet our true identity is beyond our bodies; our true identity is in that in which our bodies appear. Imagining the field of awareness in which our bodies appear, and identifying with *it* instead of with our bodies, can be a joyful thing to do.

But when I first came to nonduality, I approached it with my head. Not only was "you are not your body" a fundamental teaching, but I was never really in touch with my body in the first place, and my Catholic upbringing led me to feel it was somehow shameful in the first place.

So I avoided any practices that involved the body. Eventually, though, I realized what a wasted opportunity this was. I discovered that I couldn't jump directly to awareness without starting with what's *in* awareness right now. And the body is such a handy example of the here-and-now content of awareness. From there—

noticing the sensations in my body—I found I was then able to walk myself back to the *awareness* that noticed my body and its sensations. Looking *from* there cultivates the shift of identity from the body to pure awareness itself, and engenders that marvelous *joy of being* that this book is all about.

Motorhomes

Here's a body metaphor that's a bit on the outlandish side. It's easy to poke holes in it or dismiss it as the rambling of an overactive imagination, but it has a lot of explanatory power in terms of nondual awareness, so please humor me for a bit.

Here goes:

Imagine each of us is living in a motorhome, and we never leave the motorhome, even when we interact with each other. When we want to talk with each other, we drive up alongside another motorhome, roll down the windows and talk through them.

When we want to have sex with another individual, we park in such a way that our motorhome's reproductive apparatus (similar to tail pipes and gas tank openings) line up in the desired position.

Each motorhome is customized. Each has a unique shape, style, color, size, turning radius, fuel-efficiency rating, etc.

But as we talk and interact through our individual motorhomes, our attention is totally focused on the various characteristics of each motorhome. We don't really notice the drivers because our attention is so focused on the unique qualities of each motorhome. So much so, that we feel that we're not drivers, we *are* the motorhomes interacting with each other.

Now imagine that inside of each motorhome, there is a magical bed. A bed so comfortable that relaxation is inevitable when you lie on it. As you lie on this bed and become more and more relaxed, you can float out of your motorhome and enter a realm in which individual people can meet each other outside of their vehicles and tour each other's motorhomes.

And you realize something surprising: even though each motorhome is unique, all the other drivers look exactly like you. It's only the various makes, models, customizations, and other unique characteristics of the motorhomes that lead us into believing we're all separate from each other.

And to take it even further, as you meet the other drivers, it begins to dawn on you that not only do they all look like you—they *are* you. A you that has the ability to drive billions of individual motorhomes simultaneously.

When you rise from your magical bed and return to your motorhome, you realize that you now feel differently about all the other motorhomes. You feel more connected, more safe, more loving, knowing that the drivers are all you.

Game Break: The Body Porous
Seeing through the skin boundary.

We think of our skin as the boundary between ourselves and the world. And you don't need to stop thinking this. But you can play with the idea that it's a porous boundary. One that interacts with the air around it. One that's so open that the distinction between inside and outside completely blurs. Here's how:

- Imagine that the boundary of your skin is completely porous. Meaning that anything and everything can pass through it.
- Imagine that your skin boundary is made of air or steam or smoke. Whichever image suits you.
- Imagine that this airy boundary is utterly unaffected by anything that passes through it.
- Imagine this in all directions. Your front, back, and sides, and your above and below.
- As you breath, imagine that the air is moving in and out of your body, not only through your nose but through your entire skin. Front, back, left, right, above, below.
  - Each in-breath brings the air outside through your porous skin and into the heart of your being.
  - Each out-breath allows the core of your being to move out through your porous skin and merge with the world outside.
- Imagine that the world outside of your skin can simply pass through it, pass through your body, pass through you entirely.
- Move your arm. Imagine that as you move it, it doesn't pass through the air, the air passes through it.
- Imagine your whole body walking or moving or dancing. Imagine that, instead of moving through space, space moves through it. Space moves through you.

You can actually try this last step when you're up and moving around. If you're sitting in meditation, just imagine it.

DEEP DIVE

Happiness and Emotions

Happiness

In my first book, *Awareness Games,* I talk about that "happy for no reason" feeling that the games are designed to achieve. Yes, that feeling is available at the drop of a hat, with a little practice. But is it really a feeling? And do we need to figure out a way to feel this way all the time? Do we need to try to exclude all other feelings from our experience, particularly the so-called negative emotions like fear, loneliness, anger, anxiety, shame, and sadness? I don't think we do.

It's a paradox, but I discovered that a sure-fire way of failing to generate this happy feeling is to try to bring it about when I'm feeling otherwise. In fact, when I play an Awareness Game and fail to feel "better," I found that in every case, without exception, the reason is one of two things: I'm trying to create a desired feeling or I'm trying to stop feeling an undesired emotion.

As soon as I realize this and stop trying to change how I'm feeling right now, but instead, drop my attention to the awareness in which the feeling is appearing, I instantly get that "happy for no reason" feeling, even if I'm still feeling bad. In fact, for me, it's absolutely essential to drop all internal clutching against a negative feeling and not only completely allow it to be here, but even dive into it and allow myself to feel it fully. Being the background awareness at the same time helps to do this. Noticing what else appears in awareness right now helps to do this. Relaxing physically helps to do this. I find I can be happy while I'm sad, angry, anxious. That's the glorious paradox.

Why? Because the background awareness already allows every feeling to be here. It doesn't discriminate between good feelings and bad, between happy and sad events. It simply notices everything without judgement. This is unconditional love, and it's already happening in some part of you right now, all the time. All you have to do is notice it. And unconditional love is happiness, and happiness is our true nature already. Not something we have to bring about, but simply something we have to notice.

Another reason happiness is awareness's natural state is that awareness has no idea that anything should be different—there is nothing to get rid of and nothing is missing, which means it has no sense of lack. No sense of lack = happiness.

So happiness is not something we get from the outside world, and not something that requires the absence of negative emotions or events. It's simply our true nature as the screen or whiteboard on which all experience appears.

Have your feelings. Have them fully. Notice what is aware of them. Be that awareness.

Emotions

There is another crucial reason to have your feelings. When you don't, they get stuck inside, like internal eddies spinning endlessly and churning away, eroding your sense of well-being. These eddies have been building up and multiplying for many years, ever since your first clumsy childhood strategy to prevent pain and fear. And they draw attention to themselves by their very spinning, and distract us from the simple reality of being, thereby veiling our true nature as happiness itself.

Bringing emotions to awareness as they arise is the key to prevent new eddies from forming, and it enables us to let go of the clutching and other strategies that we employ in order to prevent unwanted emotions. This allowing and letting go leads to a life of greater ease, fluidity, and happiness.

But what about the old eddies? The ancient patterns of past emotions that are stuck inside? How about them? The answer is, we need to give them a little help. A little boost to nudge them free and allow them to surface so that they can bask in the light of pure awareness. However, since we have been so effective at preventing them from surfacing, they're pretty well hidden in the dark crevices of our inner ocean floor. We have to dive deep.

I spent half my life devising strategies to never ever again have what I called "the feeling." It was an almost undefinable mixture of shame, anger, helplessness, and fear. Shame that I was bad, fear that my parents would reject me, anger that I couldn't get the help that I needed. It was forged in the furnace of early childhood trauma (none of which was intentional on my parents' part, by the way. They were simply being human, reacting to their own physical and emotional challenges and conditioning). So the whirling patterns of pain were deep and seemingly hard-wired.

Psychotherapy was a big help. For the first time, I was able to share my emotions with someone who valued them, who was comfortable with them, who encouraged their expression. This released a great deal of the steam, and possibly saved my life. Later I came to realize that depression is not a separate emotion, it's the result of our refusal to have our emotions. It's a clamping down of our self-expression in the hope that those huge scary feelings won't be given the chance to show their horrifying faces. But it's a losing strategy because you end up having the bad feelings anyway, and on top of that, you're withholding your gifts from the world and yourself by imprisoning your natural personality, your you-ness.*

But psychotherapy didn't go far enough, at least not in my case. Perhaps it was the style of therapy prevalent at that time or the practice adhered to by my therapist, but I felt he wasted too much time passively waiting for me to bring up the emotion, when what I wanted was a teacher and a facilitator who could show me how to do the deep dive needed to dredge them up to the surface. I understand that this might have scared me away at first, but after years of therapy, I was ready. However, I was not given the tools nor taught how to use them.

---

* Note: I'm speaking here of the individual persona, the natural personality that colors each unique expression of universal awareness, which is our true nature. The individual expression can be treasured and nurtured, however, while at the same time realizing that it is not who we ultimately are.

So I recommend therapy to anyone who feels at risk of depression or worse. And if your therapist is trained in nondual approaches, all the better. But you can help the process along, or continue the process post-therapy.

My Guides, Sherpas, Trailblazers, and Master Teachers

I owe so much to several wise teachers who undoubtedly helped me navigate the treacherous waters of emotion. In this section, I'd like to offer some specific post-therapy insights and techniques from them that helped loosen the deep primal calcified emotions for me.

Inner Voice Dialogue

One mode of therapy that I *did* find helpful was Inner Voice Dialogue, also known as The Psychology of Selves, pioneered by Hal and Sidra Stone. I worked with Bridgit Dengel Gaspard, a leading Inner Voice Dialogue practitioner, who works with primary and disowned selves—parts of our personalities who have varying and often conflicting aims and goals in our lives. Bridgit talks to and engages with the different selves, as the client moves to different physical spots in the room. One sub-personality we worked with was a defiant and adamant self, who gave voice to something deep that I had never acknowledged consciously: "If I spend all my time and energy focusing on my weaknesses and flaws, I'll have nothing left to express my strengths and talents." In other words, If I only concentrate on fixing what's wrong with me, the world will miss out on what's right with me.

The other element of Inner Voice Dialogue that makes it very compatible with awareness practices is that of returning to awareness as the neutral observing self, in which all the different sub-personalities can be seen from a more spacious vantage point, and thereby accepted, allowed, and integrated.

Allowing the Feeling

One deep dive approach is to practice dissolving resistance to the feelings. When unwanted emotions come up, Rupert Spira advises that you allow the feeling without resistance. "If we replace the impulse to avoid uncomfortable feelings with a desire to face and explore them deeply, we find, at their heart, exactly what we were seeking by trying to avoid them."

Here's Rupert describing the process:

> Don't do what the feeling is asking you to do. What the feeling is asking you to do is avoid it or suppress it. Don't do either. Do the opposite. Turn around and face it. Let the feeling come totally to you. And face it so fully that you can keep facing it, keep living with the feeling, opening yourself to the feeling, until you can truly say that there is not the slightest resistance to it. And you have to be very careful, because of course, the separate self will turn even this into a technique for getting rid of the feeling. In other words, "I'm allowing the feeling so that I can get rid of it." That's not allowing the feeling. So you have to really take time and check with yourself that the feeling is being allowed without the slightest resistance to it. And the test of that is, you say to yourself, "Can I live with this feeling forever?" You have to be able to answer "yes" to that question. When you can answer "yes" honestly to that question, you know there is no resistance to it. And then, turn around and look at the feeling again and see what remains of it.[iii]

Explore this approach fully and give it your all. But if saying "yes" to this question seems impossible for you at the moment, try the quick game, "Inhale the Emotion" at the end of this section. It's easy. It's quick. It works.

Emotions as Awareness-Energy

Loch Kelly has so many wonderful "glimpse practices" that helped steer me in right direction (inside, that is). One in particular, from his book, *The Way of Effortless Mindfulness,* is useful in the deep dive into our emotions.

I heartily recommend that you refer to the complete description of this practice in his book, but in summary, it's a full-circle progression from identifying with an emotion ("I am sad," for example), to separating from the emotion ("I *feel* sadness"), to seeing the emotion within awareness ("I am *aware* of feeling sadness"), to embracing the feeling ("Sadness is welcome"), to the final shift, where we see the unity of awareness and emotion ("Awareness and sadness are not separate").

As Loch elaborates:

> Pause to feel awake awareness around and within you, permeating the emotion fully, but without identifying with the emotion or rejecting it. Feel awareness-energy with emotion fully from within. Feel the awareness, the energetic aliveness, the deep stillness of presence. Notice the feeling of looking out at others and the world from this embodied, connected, open-hearted awareness.[iv]

Take a Breath

Stuart Schwartz has a marvelously compact technique for so-called unwanted emotions.

It's so utterly simple. You acknowledge that the emotion is here, and you take a breath.

Examples:

- Anger is here. Take a breath.
- Anxiety is here. Take a breath.
- Fear is here. Take a breath.

I have found this useful on so many occasions. It's like a handy pocket-sized tool you can pull out whenever you need it.

Zero Distance

Another deep dive approach from Rupert Spira is to draw your experience of suffering so close to you that there is no distance between you and the suffering. When there is no separation from it, it cannot be experienced as suffering. As Rupert explains:

> It's only possible to label something as a contraction or unpleasant if you separate yourself from it. It's only when we separate ourselves from an experience that we can label it as something. So here, we're doing the opposite. We bring the experience so close that we cannot stand back from it and know it as an object.

> If you do just that and you ask yourself, "At this zero distance from my experience, is there anything about my experience that is unpleasant? If you go deeply into an emotional contraction so that you cannot separate yourself from it, would you even know that it's a contraction? Let alone something unpleasant? You have an experience, but without referring to thought or memory, you have no idea what it is that you are experiencing other than a certain vibration.

> Take any moment of suffering and do the same experiment with your suffering. Ask yourself, without reference to thought or memory, what can I say that is true about this experience? You'll fall silent. You'll have no knowledge that you are suffering. Right there, at the very heart of your suffering, you find the peace for which you are in search. Not by moving away from the experience, but by going so fully into it that it loses its objective qualities and its pleasantness or unpleasantness. You literally cannot say

whether it's pleasant or unpleasant. You cannot say a single word about it.[v]

A third deep dive approach is to develop the skill of inviting deeply hidden emotions to the surface. Here's a technique I've worked with often and can recommend for doing that:

Navigating Negative Emotions

Adyashanti has an audio meditation called "Working with Negative Emotions"[vi] which has been a huge help for me over the years and was instrumental in clearing the path forward between losing my day job of almost 20 years and writing my first book, *Awareness Games.*

In the meditation, he points out how important it is to understand that "if you're trying to be free *of* an emotion, then you are standing in opposition to it. You're trying to control it. Instead, what we're looking at is how to free a negative emotion itself. How to grant that emotion freedom for its own well-being and your own."

He asks us to bring to mind a negative emotion that's common for us and suggests recalling some of the narrative or storyline attached to the emotion. This is to help bring the emotion vividly to the foreground of our experience. He asks us then to feel the energy of the emotion as fully as possible. But once we can fully allow ourselves to feel the emotion, Adyashanti suggests that we can then "begin to let go of the narrative; let go of the storytelling for the moment and shift all of your attention to the energy of the emotion itself—commit to the feeling of it, in your body—so that you can be absolutely intimate with the energy of it and not move from it."

But he doesn't stop there. Once you open to your emotion and begin to experience it fully, Adya suggests that you ask yourself, "What emotion or energy is deeper than this?" And keep asking as you allow yourself to feel each deeper layer of energy in your body.

Lastly, he invites you to "just let your attention relax from any experience, and let it settle just into the simple act of awareness, of being conscious... and let it all unfold into the expanse, the empty field of awareness (as) it delivers you back into the heart, into the clear and loving heart."

So we're bringing our emotions to awareness, or bringing awareness to our emotions, and as we do, the veil of emotions becomes more and more transparent, revealing the loving peaceful nature of awareness itself, as it is now and as it has always been.

If you try this practice, you can start slowly, or start with relatively less painful emotions, and gradually work towards the most overwhelming ones in your life. If you're willing to go as deep as you can, and know that without the storyline, feelings are actually just sensations in your body, you can reach down into the core wound that has shaped your life.

If it doesn't feel safe for you to go this deeply on your own, consider doing this meditation with a trusted friend or even a professional therapist.

As an example, during one of my sessions with this guided meditation, I was able to see that the core wound underneath all my other emotions, was the early childhood fear that my parents were so dangerously angry at me that they would withhold their protection, care, and love. The irrational thought, which I know now to be untrue, popped into my head: "My parents hate me." Tears poured forth as I allowed myself to have this feeling as fully as possible. Eventually, the tears subsided, and a deep sense of relief came over me, along with profound relaxation and newfound energy, as I simply allowed this feeling to be, and allowed myself to experience it as fully and deeply as possible. This is what I mean by "deep dive."

The Core Wound

Some further thoughts about the core wound...

Debbie Ford, who was a proponent of exploring and embracing the "shadow" side of ourselves, had this to say about the wounded ego:

> This is one of the most important things I can tell you: The wounded ego isn't going away. *Your* wounded ego isn't going away. And although it will try every trick in the book to have you believe otherwise, there is nothing you can do to fix it, kill it, ignore it, or bury it. You can't make it disappear by achieving, earning, educating, marrying, divorcing, dieting, or negotiating your way out of it. You can't manipulate, manage, or control it. But you can give it what it actually wants—safety, compassion, kindness, understanding, love, and reconnection with your whole self.[vii]

It's crucial to remember that we are not trying to get rid of anything—not any experience, nor any feeling, nor any parts of our personalities. We are simply giving these wounded emotions attention and love and acceptance and gratitude. Yes, even gratitude. It's counterintuitive, but crucial to realize that the parts of ourselves that engender so-called negative behaviors are based on self-love, not self-hate. These are the parts of ourselves that were created when we were very young to protect us from the overwhelming feelings and events that we were powerless over, because we were simply too young and too vulnerable.

These parts are like big dumb guards whose reasons for guarding have long since become obsolete. When an overwhelming feeling came along, they triggered protective behavior like withdrawal or lashing out, or self-soothing behavior like eating, or defensive beliefs like "I must be bad if my parents are so angry," because it's too dangerous, and in fact, impossible for a young child to believe that parents are bad, because this is a direct threat to survival.

But why do these big dumb guards install these behaviors, beliefs, and strategies? Because they want to protect us. And why do they want to protect us? Because they love us! It's just that their mission was assigned before we had the skills to master more effective strategies, and they continue, unaware that they're no longer needed.

It's astonishing to realize that all our pain is rooted in love. All of the dysfunctional, mean, cruel, or hurtful behavior in the world is misguided love. Looking for love in all the wrong places. What is the right place? Right here, right now, in the simple choiceless awareness of direct experience. It doesn't need to be found. It's already here, waiting for you to give it your attention so that it can pour forth its unconditional love in return.

It's awareness itself. It's love itself. It's you yourself.

Exploration: Include More
Putting it all in perspective

In *Awareness Games,* I included a game for dealing with tough emotions. I called it "Include, Include, Include." I described how sometimes painful emotions wash over you and demand your attention like an alarm clock, pulling your focus in, narrowing it down, as if to say "Deal with me! Don't think of anything else! Fix this!"

After playing with it and sharing it with others for some time, I came to think of it as an essential tool even when emotions *aren't* running rampant. It's an effective way of seeing present moment reality in all its many facets, instead of only the virtual reality of your narrowly focused mind. It can be applied when obsessive thoughts are taking over, or when you feel stuck in patterns of behavior, or even when you're feeling okay, and would love a little extra insight into the nature of awareness, and of yourself.

The other advantage is that it helps us to see awareness as all-encompassing. Everything is in the same single field of awareness. Awareness allows and includes everything. Awareness is made of everything. Everything is made of awareness. In other words, the more you notice and the more you include in your field of attention, the more you come to see yourself, awareness, and the universe as one intimately entwined reality.

But of course, it's really useful for those tough unwanted emotions.

The idea is to notice what the focus of your attention is right now, and then to ask yourself what else is in awareness in the present moment.

So here's how it goes:

- Just for a few seconds, don't try to change anything about your current experience. Don't try to fix anything, make anything go away, or bring about anything new.
- Ask yourself, "What am I aware of right now?

- Whatever pops into your mind first, notice it's showing up in awareness.
- Include more.
- What else is in awareness? Sounds? Sights? Sensations? Feelings? Thoughts?
- Include even more.
- Include yourself and your body.
- Include anyone else you can think of.
- Include any place you can see or imagine.
- Include even more.
- Expand awareness until it includes every possible thing.
- Notice that everything you can possibly be aware of shares that same awareness with every other possible thing you can be aware of.
- See awareness as one unlimited open spacious field.

Play with this often, and over time, you'll begin to sense the infinite and inclusive nature of awareness. You'll begin to identify with pure awareness, as you see that everything, including you, is joined by everything else in the one magnificent continuous experience of being.

And the gravy is, the tough unwanted emotion that craved all the attention now feels proportionally much smaller, as it shares the vast field of awareness with everything else that can be experienced in each moment.

The Path of Pain

It is pain that usually brings us to the spiritual search, and in fact, we often feel compelled to try anything that will get rid of pain. It's understandable and utterly human.

If we can set aside all the outward strategies that we employ to get rid of it, pain can be seen as a call from the universal consciousness, beckoning us to turn inward and seek it within, know it, and join it.

Pain is a given in life. As the saying goes, pain is mandatory; suffering is optional. Suffering is the idea that pain shouldn't *be.* It is resistance that brings suffering.

Does this mean there's no way out? No, there's hope. But once again, paradox rules the day. Letting go of hope is not the same as hopelessness. It's temporarily dropping the strategies we employ in order to make pain go away, and instead, having a willingness to dive into the pain with open curiosity—really asking what it's made of; what are its qualities; what's behind it? We may find that it's indescribable and unfathomable—and that's a good thing, because it's our concepts that produce pain. We may also find that love is the deep background to pain, for, what is pain other than a desire for us to be healthy, to be well, to be at peace? And that's love.

So sometimes the way out of pain is a path straight through it.

The best description of this path is from my friend Ron Buchheim, and so I'll close this section with Ron's words, which are far better and more vivid than I could come up with. Ron wrote this in an email response to a mutual friend who had been missing him and wondered how he was doing:

> The pain is right down the center of the chest, where the trachea and esophagus lie. The original throat infection got in there, for about the fifth prolonged bout in the past 20 years, leaving me with some mild chronic inflammation, probably tracheal, that I can hear when I cough deeply even when healthy. That was aggravated by postnasal drip from a substantial sinus infection and possibly by a "severe" dust mite allergy as well as acid reflux. I'm taking all possible steps against those conditions, but the pain lingers. I suspect that chronic inflammation doesn't go away easily. I'm taking a medicine chest full of anti-inflammatory herbs. Maybe I'll try the Chinese doctor who helped somewhat during my last chest infection. Acupuncture, Reiki, and a Tibetan healer didn't help.

But what's most interesting about this is that relaxing, letting go, and getting in touch with the love deep within *does* relieve the pain—nothing else does. So this condition, like other suffering, may be a blessing in disguise. It has forced me to stop obsessing and rushing, to let go of anger and resentment, and to return, as best I can, to the innocence and warm heartedness of childhood, as most spiritual teachings instruct. But this time it's not an idea, it's a necessity, because when I move away from that, the pain recurs. It's like a super form of biofeedback. Or like god has me in his grip and squeezes when I stray from his/her love. Purgatory?

Don't try this at home--it's not fun, though ultimately the reward may be great.

૭

Certainly, for me, when I've tried an awareness game or meditation practice with the purpose of *getting rid of* pain, it hasn't worked. Meaning, not only did I not get rid of the pain, but I didn't succeed in connecting with the joy of being awareness. In fact, connecting with the joy of being awareness only works for me if I'm totally okay with things just the way they are and I'm not trying to recreate a past good feeling, get rid of a current bad feeling, or avoid future pain.

And when I *do* let go of trying to get rid of anything, and turn my attention to awareness itself, I see that there is something within me that is already there and that does not suffer, even when pain is present.

So it's not a magic pill to make pain disappear. But the good news is, pain can be your guide to awakening to your true nature.

Game Break: Inhale the Emotion
When all else fails, try this.

If all of these approaches to emotional pain are too much for you, or too scary, or you don't have time in this moment and you need something right now, here's an easy way.

In this simple game, you don't have to get rid of an emotion, and you don't have to accept it either. You don't have to allow it, and you don't have to transform it. You don't have to convince yourself that it's okay if it never goes away.

You simply have to inhale it.

When you feel an emotion, do this:
- Notice the emotion.
- Inhale the emotion.
- Repeat as needed.

You don't even have to worry about *exhaling* the emotion, because that might feel like you're trying to get rid of it. In this game, you're not trying to get rid of it. You're not trying to do anything with it other than inhale it—draw it into you.

Simple as that. Inhale the emotion.

JOURNEY'S END

The Ultimate Exploration

This is the ultimate meditation in the book because it includes the deepest and most recent insights that I've stumbled upon, and it has become my go-to, when-in-doubt, this-is-it, if-you-could-only-pick-one meditative exploration.

It's playing with the idea that what you think of as "myself" is no different from sounds, sensations, thoughts, or anything else that appears in that unnamable concept-free beingness that is all that is. Your sense of yourself is just another thought. Or, for the sake of this meditation, you can think of it as like a thought, in that it's just another appearance in awareness. It appears simultaneously in the same clear field of awareness as sounds, sensations, perceptions, thoughts, emotions, and anything else that you could possibly experience. In this field of awareness there are no borders or boundaries between any of these; it's all one taste—and it's what you are: not a thing, but simply "experiencing."

Meditation: Quintangulation
Sounds plus Sensations plus Visual Field plus Thoughts plus Sense of Self

This meditation builds upon the earlier two, "Triangulation" and "Quadrangulation," by adding a fifth element—your sense of yourself. That is, what your mind tells you "I" is.

As with the Triangulation and Quadrangulation meditations, we are experiencing the all-inclusiveness of awareness by noticing that more than one mode of experience appears in the same field of awareness at the same time. But this time, we're experimenting to see if you can realize that your sense of yourself as a separate identity is simply another element that appears in awareness, along with sound, body sensations, sights, and thoughts.

If you haven't tried the Triangulation and Quadrangulation meditations, I recommend you try them first, and when you get a good intuitive feel of those, move on to this one.

Here's the Quintangulation meditation:

- Starting with your eyes closed, listen to the sounds around you—the hum of an air conditioner or heater, or perhaps the sounds of traffic or birds or wind outside, or the sound of my voice.
    - As you notice the sounds that appear, ask yourself, "What is the silent field in which the sounds appear?"
    - Notice each sound separately, and ask the question, "What is the silent field in which this sound appears?"
    - Now see if you can notice all the sounds at the same time, and ask yourself, "Do all the sounds appear in the same silent field?"
- Then notice your bodily sensations—the feel of your body on the chair, or your feet on the floor. Perhaps a breeze on your skin, or the rise and fall of your belly as you breathe.
    - As you notice the sensations that appear, ask yourself, "What is the empty spacious field in which sensations appear?"
    - Notice each sensation separately, and ask the question, "What is the empty spacious field in which this sensation appears?"
    - Now see if you can notice all the sensations at the same time, and ask yourself, "Do all these sensations appear in the same empty spacious field?"
- Now see if you can notice both sounds and body sensations at the same time.
    - Ask yourself, "Is the field in which sounds appear, the same as the field in which sensations appear?" This is the clear field of awareness.
- Notice what thoughts are appearing now.

- o Imagine the thoughts are coming from somewhere outside of you and are projected on a blank screen inside you.
- o Imagine that the screen has both sound and subtitles, so you can either hear or read each thought that appears.
- o Imagine this screen is like a clear empty field in which thoughts appear.
- o As you notice the thoughts that appear, ask yourself, "what is the blank empty field in which these thoughts appear?"
- o Notice a few thoughts separately, as they appear in a sequence of thoughts, and for each one, ask yourself, "Do all these thoughts appear in the same empty field?"
- Now see if you can notice both the thoughts and the body sensation at the same time.
  - o Ask yourself, "Is the field in which thoughts appear, the same as the field in which sensations appear?"
- Then see if you can notice both the thoughts and the sounds at the same time.
  - o Ask yourself, "Is the field in which thoughts appear, the same as the field in which sounds appear?"
    - Now see if you can notice all three—the sounds, the sensations, and the thoughts—appearing at the same time, and ask yourself, "Are these all appearing in the same clear empty field of awareness?"
- Keeping your eyes closed, notice what colors or patterns or shapes are appearing behind your eyelids. This is your visual field, which is still present even if your eyes are closed.
  - o As you notice the visual field and the colors and shapes that appear, ask yourself, "what is the blank empty field in which these colors and shapes appear?"
- Now see if you can notice both the visual images and the body sensation at the same time.

- o Ask yourself, "Is the field in which visual images appear, the same as the field in which sensations appear?"
- Now see if you can notice both the visual images and the sounds at the same time.
  - o Ask yourself, "Is the field in which visual images appear, the same as the field in which sounds appear?"
- Then see if you can notice both the visual images and thoughts at the same time.
  - o Ask yourself, "Is the field in which visual images appear, the same as the field in which thoughts appear?"
    - Now see if you can notice all four—the sounds, the sensations, the thoughts, and the visual images— appearing at the same time, and ask yourself, "Are these all appearing in the same clear empty field of awareness?"
- Think the thought, "I." Notice what appears in your mind.
  - o It doesn't matter if it's an image, a feeling, or a concept, I'm talking about the felt sense of being yourself. Whatever it is that you're referring to when you say "I."
- Now see if you can notice all five—the sounds, the sensations, the visual images, the thoughts, and the sense of "I"—appearing at the same time, and ask yourself, "Are these all appearing in the same clear empty field of awareness?"
- Notice that in the open field of awareness, there are no borders or boundaries among any of these. No borders between thoughts, images, sounds, sensations, or your sense of yourself. They are all simultaneously appearing in one indivisible field of awareness.
- That field is your true nature. Clear, spacious, silent, allowing,
- Be that field. It's who you really are, so might as well be that knowingly.

- Now, if your eyes are closed, gently open them again and take another easy breath.

My hope is that you will see, or rather feel into the non-conceptual knowing that your sense of yourself as a separate entity is simply another appearance in the indivisible field of awareness— the real you.

RETURNING HOME

Get Off the Information Highway

Information flows in one direction from the world, through the mind, to universal awareness. All thought is simply adding more information to the flow. Getting involved in the information by analyzing, figuring out, conceptualizing, strategizing, acquiring, or preventing, only adds to the one-way current of information flowing through the mind to universal awareness.

All experience, including sensations and perceptions, is information flowing through the mind into universal awareness. The sense of oneself as an individual is information located in the mind, and is part of the flow of information.

Universal awareness is that which receives the flow of information.

The information flows through a one-way door from the mind into universal consciousness or awareness. Universal awareness receives the flow of information from all individual doors simultaneously.

But there are two doors, metaphorically, like the in and the out doors between a restaurant's dining room and its kitchen. However, for most of us, the door that opens from universal awareness into the individual mind is firmly closed.

Turning attention from the information to the receiver of the information, that is, awareness itself, opens the other door—the one that flows from universal awareness back into the individual mind and body.

The more we ignore the information and instead, turn our attention to the receiver or knower of the information, the stronger the current that flows through this second door. The one-way flow becomes a two-way flow.

But what is it that flows from universal awareness into the individual body and mind? It is not information. It does not communicate in the same language as what flows into it through the mind. It communicates in feeling, for lack of a better word, and it flows directly into the heart.

And what is it that it communicates through feeling? It communicates its own nature. That of peaceful, allowing, and unconditional love, which is its nature because it contains no divisions between good and bad, between acceptable and unacceptable, desirable and undesirable.

If this flow of feeling, this perfume that wafts into the heart from universal awareness, did not flow into the individual, we would not experience the joy and peace of enlightenment, in which case, what good would enlightenment be?

There is an advantage to the individual that comes with this enlightened flow, because the individual can now interact with the world of form in a way that is in keeping with—that reflects—the joy and peace that is inherent in universal awareness, which is the ultimate knower of experience, and therefore, our true self.

And when we act in a way that is in keeping with the nature of awareness itself, we start to see others as not separate from us in essence. And this creates compassion, which leads to harmony and a decrease in resistance, which in turn, leads to a sympathetic vibration with reality, which in turn, decreases suffering and increases happiness in us and in everyone we come into contact with.

If you sense yourself trying to figure this out or analyze it logically, you are getting wrapped up in the information and only increasing the one-way flow. You're using the wrong tool. You're looking in the wrong place. Instead, turn your attention around from the content of awareness to awareness itself and allow the other door to open a crack. The more you do so, the wider the crack will become, and the more the joy and peace of awareness can flow into your heart.

Once that door is open, you can step through it, know yourself as that universal awareness, and turn back around, *as* that, and see the world of form--including your body and mind—from Awareness, your true nature.

The Inward Path and the Outward Path

Rupert Spira often talks about the inward facing path and the outward facing path, and the need for both.

Much of this book describes the inward path—that is, turning your attention from the content of awareness, to look at awareness itself and explore its actual nature. When we do this, we realize that awareness is clear, choiceless, allowing, without borders or limits, and without a beginning or ending in time. We can experience it as pure love, or joy, or simply peace.

But I also encourage you to turn around and look out at the world from there—from the awareness that you are, and really see if anything out there is separate from awareness. There is nothing you or anyone else could possibly experience without awareness, so awareness is the common element of all experience. As such, all experience is pervaded by awareness; or to take it a step further, is *made of* awareness.

So, if awareness is what knows all of your experience, and is therefore you, and if all that can be experienced—including you, your body, your mind, and the so-called outside world—is made of awareness, that makes you and the world made of the same indivisible stuff.

Which means that there is only awareness (or consciousness if you prefer), and that's you. You are all; all is you.

If you discover the unconditional love that is the very nature of awareness, which is you, and you see the world as having the self-same nature, then you will see the world as love, and you—the temporary individual whirlpool of personality, will interact with the world in the same spirit of unconditional love. You will be living life in the outer world of form in accordance with the inner understanding of the formless unity.

You could say there are two you's: You, the universe, is experiencing itself through you, the temporary whirlpool of an individual. Which means of course that there aren't two you's after all. The indescribable beauty of paradox in action again.

So the inward path leads to the outward path. The self is other. There is no actual separation. The nature of the universe is love.

If we explore both directions, inward and outward, we end up in the same place—pure experience—pure awareness—pure love. So it's a circle—the inward path and the outward path meet, and merge into the pathless path. I wish you a pleasant non-voyage!

Dorothy's Discovery

By now I hope you see that this adventure is not a voyage to distant lands, even to distant lands of philosophy or spirituality. It's a voyage you undertake without going anywhere. It's a discovery that the happiness you seek is always here, always now, in what you truly are—awareness itself.

The self that is pure awareness never lets you down. It's always available. All you have to do is notice it—and notice it often enough that the noticing becomes second nature. What are you noticing when you're noticing awareness? You are noticing joy. You are noticing unconditional love. You are noticing oneness. You are noticing the only true home there is. You are noticing you.

Come home. You never actually left.

APPENDIX A: 190 METHODS PLUS ONE

Recently, I had an email exchange with Jonathan Robinson, my friend and co-host on our *Awareness Explorers* podcast. I had just finished reading the book, *The Yoga of Consciousness: 25 Direct Practices to Enlightenment* by SantataGamana, and knowing that Jonathan is a self-described method junkie, I thought a book that contained 25 different methods or practices would interest him. But my email to him contained a typo. I wrote, "Chapter 16, 'Practicing Non-Duality,' indeed has *215* methods, similar to *Awareness Games.*"

When I discovered my mistake, I wrote back, "Correction: 25 Methods (not 215). Typo."

Jonathan responded, "Damn! I almost had a spontaneous orgasm when I saw 215."

I replied, "Oops. But the 25 are choice. And I like the writing. So it's still worth it."

But Jonathan had already eagerly purchased the book, and so he wrote back, "That's all fine and good, but can you come up with the other 190 methods that you just 'took' from me?"

"Well, the title is *25 Direct Practices...* after all," I replied, "But I think I can come up with 190 more." We were joking around with each other of course, but I couldn't resist the challenge of coming up with 190 practices, just for fun.

So here goes...

190 Methods

1.   Notice Awareness.
2.   Become aware of awareness.
3.   Be awareness.
4.   Be consciousness.
5.   Ask yourself, "Who am I?"

6. Ask yourself, "What is this 'me'?"
7. Ask yourself, "Who's experiencing this?"
8. Notice your body. Ask "Who has a body?"
9. Be the background.
10. Take a half step back in your mind and be that which sees.
11. Be the witness.
12. Ask yourself, "who hears this sound?"
13. Ask yourself, "who has this thought?"
14. Ask yourself, "Where does this thought come from?"
15. Ask yourself, "Did I decide to have this thought?"
16. Ask yourself, "What is the Self?"
17. Ask yourself, "Am I my hand?"
18. Ask yourself, "Am I my torso?"
19. Ask yourself, "Am I my head?"
20. Ask yourself, "Am I my body"
21. Ask yourself, "Am I my mind?"
22. Notice present experience.
23. Ask yourself, "Am I aware?"
24. Ask yourself, "How do I know I'm aware?"
25. Ask yourself, "Is it possible to *not* be aware?"
26. Try to step away from yourself.
27. Ignore all thoughts about the past.
28. Ignore all thoughts about the future.
29. Shift your attention from the content of awareness to awareness itself.
30. Shift your attention from what you're looking at to what's looking.
31. Notice if the sounds you hear and the sensations in your body appear in the same field of awareness.
32. Imagine you are bigger than your body, looking at your body from outside of it.
33. Imagine all you experience is made of awareness.
34. Notice what's in your experience other than words in your head.
35. Ignore all thought.

36.   Notice if the sights you see and the thoughts in your mind appear in the same field of awareness.
37.   See if there are many awarenesses or just one.
38.   Examine the nature of awareness: Does it have a shape?
39.   Examine the nature of awareness: Does it have qualities?
40.   Examine the nature of awareness: Does it have dimensions?
41.   Examine the nature of awareness: Does it have limits?
42.   Examine the nature of awareness: Does it appear in time?
43.   Notice what has not changed since you were a little child.
44.   Notice what's noticing.
45.   Notice what's experiencing.
46.   Notice what's feeling.
47.   Notice noticing.
48.   Instead of objects being outside of you, imagine objects are experienced within you.
49.   Instead of awareness being in you, imagine you are in awareness.
50.   Allow everything to be as it is.
51.   Don't have any intention.
52.   Do nothing.
53.   Just be.
54.   See your body and mind as empty of separate existence.
55.   See that only you, universal consciousness, have existence.
56.   Be the silence in which sounds appear.
57.   Be the space in which objects appear.
58.   Be the emptiness in which thoughts appear.
59.   Be the eternal now in which time appears.
60.   Imagine there is nothing.
61.   Imagine there is only one thing.
62.   Notice what already accepts everything.
63.   Notice what already loves unconditionally.
64.   Be that acceptance.
65.   Be that love.
66.   Love unconditionally.
67.   Allow thoughts to come and go.
68.   Allow feelings to come and go.

69.   Allow experiences to come and go.
70.   Do not hold on to anything.
71.   Let go of resistance to any thought.
72.   Let go of resistance to any feeling.
73.   Let go of resistance to any experience.
74.   Relax and be still.
75.   Allow your heart to open.
76.   Let your body's edges become soft.
77.   Let your body's edges become translucent.
78.   Let your body's edges become porous.
79.   Expand your boundaries as far as you can imagine.
80.   Be a river, and float downstream.
81.   Be a mirror and reflect everything choicelessly.
82.   Know knowingness.
83.   Be knowingness alone.
84.   Shift your identity from the body to what's aware of the body.
85.   Shift your identity from the mind to what's aware of the mind.
86.   Shift your identity from your name to what knows your name.
87.   Imagine you were just born.
88.   Imagine you know no language.
89.   Imagine what's looking out through your eyes is identical to what's looking out through everyone else's eyes.
90.   Imagine what's looking out through your eyes is *the same thing* as what's looking out through everyone else's eyes.
91.   See your body as an action figure.
92.   See your body and mind as a camera. Be the photographer behind it.
93.   See your body and mind as robot. Be the controller behind it.
94.   See your body and mind as a Mars rover. Be Mission Control.
95.   See your ego as a temporary whirlpool in a river, and dissolve back into the river.
96.   Ask, "Is awareness ever not present?"
97.   Notice that awareness is aware.

98. Notice that awareness is aware effortlessly.
99. Use the least amount of effort possible to keep your attention on awareness itself.
100. Shift your attention from virtual reality of the past and future to real reality of the present.
101. Be Now. Be Here. Be This.
102. See the world as appearing within you.
103. See the world as you.
104. Be the passenger to your experience.
105. Allow fear to be here.
106. Allow anxiety to be here.
107. Allow sadness to be here.
108. Know that fear is only trying to protect you.
109. Know that anxiety is only trying to protect you.
110. Know that sadness is only trying to protect you.
111. Thank the fear for protecting you.
112. Thank the anxiety for protecting you.
113. Thank the sadness for protecting you.
114. Notice what's noticing your breathing.
115. Allow everyone else to be as they are.
116. Know that everyone does what is in their nature to do.
117. Forgive everyone.
118. Forgive yourself.
119. Free the world from your expectations.
120. Say "yes" to everything.
121. What do you experience without analyzing?
122. What do you experience without concepts?
123. Be the screen that experience appears on.
124. Be the blank canvas that experience is painted on.
125. Be the blank page that words are written on.
126. Be the blank whiteboard that diagrams are drawn on.
127. Find out if you choose your thoughts.
128. Notice what is already happy.
129. See if you can stay with "Now. Here. This" without stepping away into past memory or imagined future.

130. Ask yourself, "Would I know I'm not enlightened without consulting the past?"
131. Imagine happiness wasn't something to get.
132. Imagine happiness wasn't something that comes from outside or arrives from elsewhere.
133. Imagine happiness wasn't something to pursue, or to hope will happen sometime in the future.
134. Imagine happiness was something that's already here, inside each of us, just waiting, hoping to be noticed.
135. Imagine happiness was our natural state, simply obscured by our thoughts about fixing, changing, improving.
136. Imagine happiness was our true self, informed by the unconditional choiceless acceptance of all that is.
137. What if all we have to do is notice it?
138. Instead of thinking of it as becoming happy, think of it as becoming happiness. Notice that we already are happiness.
139. Ask, "Is the sky affected by clouds?"
140. Ask, "Is the sky affected by birds?"
141. Be the sky, not the clouds.
142. Be the sky, not the birds.
143. Ask, "Is awareness affected by anything that appears in it?"
144. Be the awareness, not what appears in it.
145. Then be everything that appears as well. Because it's all made of awareness.
146. What if the body and mind are universal consciousness's drones, sent forth into the world to record images and sounds and transmit them back to universal consciousness?
147. What if consciousness was not local?
148. Know that you are doing the best you possibly can.
149. How do you know what's supposed to happen? Look at what's happening. That's what's supposed to happen.
150. Surrender control.
151. Let go of trying to change your experience.
152. Let go of trying to fix yourself.
153. Let go of trying to fix others.
154. Let go of trying to fix the world.

155. Turn your attention to the sense of "I Am."
156. Abide as "I am."
157. Abide as pure awareness.
158. Be pure subjectivity.
159. Be the "Big I," not the "Little Me."
160. When listening to others, listen from awareness, not from the judging or planning mind.
161. When listening to music, imagine it arising and appearing within you.
162. When in nature, imagine yourself as part of nature.
163. Imagine there is no separation between you and everything else.
164. See that nothing is permanent. Except awareness.
165. See that nothing is perfect. Except awareness.
166. See that nothing is complete. Except awareness.
167. When riding in a car, bus, plane, or train, imagine that, instead of you moving through your environment, imagine your environment moving through you.
168. When moving your hand through the air, imagine that it's simply pixels changing color.
169. Ask yourself, "Has anything you've ever experienced—or could ever experience—happened outside of awareness?"
170. Every time you feel a negative emotion, ask "What is this appearing in?"
171. Every time you feel a negative emotion, be the pure awareness that sees it.
172. Find out what thought is made of.
173. Find out whether thought happens by itself.
174. See how long you can go without words going through your mind.
175. Ask, "Does the past exist without thought?"
176. Ask, "What if I completely forgot my story? Would I be the same person?
177. When thoughts come, don't let them linger; let them slide out the other side.
178. See that consciousness is all there is.

179. See that all there is is consciousness.
180. Let go of all effort.
181. Repeat your name over and over until it loses all meaning.
182. See that all is well.
183. See that all is one.
184. See that all is you.
185. Imagine the universe looking at itself through a little window of your face.
186. Imagine the universe looking at itself through seven billion little windows of eyes.
187. Imagine the "million-eyed mind."
188. See the universe as you.
189. Know that God is looking out through your eyes at himself.
190. Be.

One Method

That is, all methods in a nutshell

- Allow whatever is arising right now to be just as it is, without any attempt to change it.
  - Without any attempt to understand it, describe it, label it, or improve it.
  - Without any attempt to get rid of anything, or to bring about anything.
- Turn your attention from the content of awareness to awareness itself.
- Turn around again and *be* awareness itself, looking at the world and at yourself.
- See that no experience is outside of awareness.
  - In other words, you are all, all is you, you are awareness, all is awareness.
- Rest as that.

Rest As Awareness.

APPENDIX B: LIST OF METHODS BY TYPE AND LENGTH

Sometimes you only have a minute or two and you'd like to pop into being awareness. Other times, you have plenty of time and would like to marinate in the deep peace and joy of your true nature.

Below is a list of all the stuff in this book that you can try yourself, sorted by how long each takes.

SHORT: GAMES

The shortest type of method are the games. You can do these anytime anywhere, for as long or as short as you like.

MEDIUM: EXPLORATIONS

The explorations are like longer games. Take the time to explore for yourself, but as with games, you can do these anytime, anywhere, for as long or as short as you like.

LONGER: MEDITATIONS

The meditations are usually longer and are more or less of fixed length. But you can take as long as you like to pause between the steps or the questions in each meditation.

Here's what I recommend:

Try as many out as interest you. Then pick one short one to do several times a day for a week or two. And also pick one longer one to do once a day for a week or two. If you like them, stick with them. If not, try others. But give each a chance.

ACKNOWLEDGEMENTS

Thanks so much to all those who read drafts of this book and gave invaluable feedback: Lindsay Stern, Jonathan Robinson, Glynnis O'Connor, and Bridgit Dengel Gaspard. Thanks to Jamie Watters and Anthony Holdampf, who encouraged me to write a second book in the first place. To Ron Buchheim for his wisdom and humor, and for generously allowing me to quote him in the book. Thanks to Jonathan Robinson, my co-host on the *Awareness Explorers* podcast—where several of the meditations in this book first made an appearance—for the joyful and inspiring collaboration we share. Thanks to my mom, Lenka Peterson O'Connor, whom we lost last year, and who decades and decades ago was way ahead of the curve and introduced me to such marvelous books as *How to Meditate, Cosmic Consciousness, Handbook to Higher Consciousness, A Course in Miracles,* and *The Lazy Man's Guide to Enlightenment.* Thanks also to these folks for their warm support and encouragement: Fred Adams, Monica Hoyt, Dana Chang—who has also been the generous host of the Awareness Games Meetup—and my fabulous husband, Josh Yu.

Thanks also go to the gang at the *Rupert Spira NY Non-Duality Group* meetup, including hosts Walter and Patricia, Jacques, Jane, Lalita, Eric, John, Matt, Vita, Tara, Jimmy, Bou, Wing, Ron, Alix, Barbara, Billie, Jacques, Jamie, Amy, Andi, Abhit, Annelie, Al, Mahsa, Phil, Pierre, Annette, Desmond, Tat, Kevin, Jean, Jessica, Holger, Chris, Inguna, George, Nicolle, Walter C, Jack, Fran, Nikola, Judy, Ela, Judith, Jeffrey, Robert, Dan, and Yosef, among many others.

Thanks to all the wonderful folks who have attended the live *Awareness Games* meetup and helped me with invaluable game-testing and feedback, including Elisabeth, Andrei, Lalita, Jane, Hervé, Barbara, Daniela, Yong, Yuliya, Vivek, Ron, Josh, John, Eric, Vita, Patricia, Billie, Tara, Glynnis, Selena, Jimmy, Kim, Slawek, Akshay, Joshua, Maria, Rachel, Nelson, Elaf, Fathima, Yogesh, Javier, Monica, Michael, Michelle, and many more.

And finally, I have learned such a great deal from these wonderful teachers: Stuart Schwartz, Pamela Wilson, and Loch Kelly (all of whom I was able to work with in person) and Rupert Spira, Adyashanti, and Angelo DiLullo (through their books, videos, public appearances, and as guests on Jonathan's and my podcast). As I wrote in my first book, even though I owe a debt of gratitude to these teachers, I make no claim to have attained some sort of special state that they may have attained. Nor do I claim that they have somehow anointed, designated, or authorized me to pass on their teachings. They haven't, and I haven't asked them to. The only claim I can make is that I'm ten times happier than I used to be, and that I owe this to applying these types of teachings while directly looking within.

RECOMMENDED READING AND VIEWING

Awareness Explorers podcast
https://www.awarenessexplorers.com/

Adyashanti
Emptiness Dancing by Adyashanti, Sounds True, 2004, 2006
True Meditation: Discover the Freedom of Pure Awareness by
Adyashanti, Sounds True, 2006
https://www.adyashanti.org/

Loch Kelly
*Shift into Freedom: The Science and Practice of Open-Hearted
Awareness* by Loch Kelly, Sounds True, 2015
*The Way of Effortless Mindfulness: A Revolutionary Guide for Living
an Awakened Life,* by Loch Kelly, Sounds True, 2019
https://lochkelly.org/

Stuart Schwartz
http://www.satsangwithstuart.com/

Rupert Spira
Being Aware of Being Aware, by Rupert Spira, Sahaja Publications,
2017
https://non-duality.rupertspira.com/home

Angelo DiLullo
Awake: It's Your Turn, by Angelo DiLullo, SimplyAlwaysAwake.com,
2021
http://simplyalwaysawake.com/

Bridgit Dengel Gaspard
The Final Eighth by Bridgit Dengel Gaspard, New World Library,
2020
https://www.final8th.com/

Jonathan Robinson
The Enlightenment Project: How I Went From Depressed to Blessed, and You Can Too, by Jonathan Robinson, 2022
https://findinghappiness.com/

ABOUT THE AUTHOR

Brian Tom O'Connor is the author of *Awareness Games: Playing With your Mind to Create Joy,* and is the co-host, with Jonathan Robinson, of the podcast, *Awareness Explorers.* He is also a singer, cabaret performer, and musical theater nerd. And more importantly, he's a formerly depressed guy who stumbled into the infinite well of joy lying at the heart of all experience, and who loves to share this discover with anyone who is interested.

ENDNOTES

---

[i] David R. Hawkins, *The Eye of the I: From Which Nothing Is Hidden,* Hay House Inc. (2016)

[ii] Loch Kelly, Effortless Mindfulness Now, Audible (2017)
https://www.audible.com/pd/Effortless-Mindfulness-Now-Audiobook/B074GFJZ76?qid=1603122144&sr=1-1&ref=a_search_c3_lProduct_1_1&pf_rd_p=e81b7c27-6880-467a-b5a7-13cef5d729fe&pf_rd_r=NECCNYE2DVBY6Y0JNRHG

[iii] From the Rupert Spira video, "Exploring Uncomfortable Feelings"
https://www.youtube.com/watch?v=dUR_CqH7kO8

[iv] Loch Kelly, *The Way of Effortless Mindfulness,* Sounds True (2019)
https://www.amazon.com/gp/product/B07FDR6M2T/ref=dbs_a_def_rwt_bibl_v_ppi_i0

[v] From Rupert Spira "A Body Pervaded by Peace" from the Seven Day Retreat at Mercy Center, CA, 31st October 2018 (PM)
https://non-duality.rupertspira.com/listen/a-body-pervaded-by-peace

[vi] Adyashanti, GUIDED MEDITATIONS: Evoking the Divine Ground of Your Being
Sounds True, October 01, 2015
ISBN-10: 1-62203-583-6
ISBN-13: 978-1-62203-583-0
PRODUCT CODE: AW04545W
https://www.soundstrue.com/store/guided-meditations.html

[vii] Debbie Ford, "Overcoming Self Sabotage" from DailyOM
https://www.dailyom.com/cgi-bin/courses/courseoverview.cgi?cid=15&aff=&co=

CPSIA information can be obtained
at www.ICGtesting.com
Printed in the USA
LVHW011146091222
734844LV00001B/103

9 780578 892108